LIFE OUT OF DEATH

Life Out of Death

A Thought a Day for the Easter Season

HAROLD A. BUETOW, PHD, JD

ST PAULS

Alba
House

Library of Congress Cataloging-in-Publication Data

Buetow, Harold A.
    Life out of death : a thought a day for the Easter season / Harold A. Buetow.
        p. cm.
    ISBN 0-8189-0965-X
1. Lenten sermons. 2. Easter—Sermons. 3. Catholic Church—Sermons.
4. Bible—Sermons. I. Title.

    BV4277.B78 2005
    252'.63—dc22
                              2004003996

Produced and designed in the United States of America by the
Fathers and Brothers of the Society of St. Paul,
2187 Victory Boulevard, Staten Island, NY 10314-6603,
as part of their communications apostolate.

ISBN: 0-8189-0965-X

Printing Information:

Current Printing - first digit	1	2	3	4	5	6	7	8	9	10

Year of Current Printing - first year shown

2005	2006	2007	2008	2009	2010	2011	2012	2013	2014

Though words are in the final analysis
empty in giving thanks, I would like to extend
the depth of my gratitude in this work for the
kindness and graciousness given by
Dr. Rose M. Auteri,
Patricia C. Deeley,
Steven Krogman, and
Col. (Ret.) Michael L. Wardinski, Ph.D.

Biblical Abbreviations

OLD TESTAMENT

Genesis	Gn	Nehemiah	Ne	Baruch	Ba
Exodus	Ex	Tobit	Tb	Ezekiel	Ezk
Leviticus	Lv	Judith	Jdt	Daniel	Dn
Numbers	Nb	Esther	Est	Hosea	Ho
Deuteronomy	Dt	1 Maccabees	1 M	Joel	Jl
Joshua	Jos	2 Maccabees	2 M	Amos	Am
Judges	Jg	Job	Jb	Obadiah	Ob
Ruth	Rt	Psalms	Ps	Jonah	Jon
1 Samuel	1 S	Proverbs	Pr	Micah	Mi
2 Samuel	2 S	Ecclesiastes	Ec	Nahum	Na
1 Kings	1 K	Song of Songs	Sg	Habakkuk	Hab
2 Kings	2 K	Wisdom	Ws	Zephaniah	Zp
1 Chronicles	1 Ch	Sirach	Si	Haggai	Hg
2 Chronicles	2 Ch	Isaiah	Is	Malachi	Ml
Ezra	Ezr	Jeremiah	Jr	Zechariah	Zc
		Lamentations	Lm		

NEW TESTAMENT

Matthew	Mt	Ephesians	Eph	Hebrews	Heb
Mark	Mk	Philippians	Ph	James	Jm
Luke	Lk	Colossians	Col	1 Peter	1 P
John	Jn	1 Thessalonians	1 Th	2 Peter	2 P
Acts	Ac	2 Thessalonians	2 Th	1 John	1 Jn
Romans	Rm	1 Timothy	1 Tm	2 John	2 Jn
1 Corinthians	1 Cor	2 Timothy	2 Tm	3 John	3 Jn
2 Corinthians	2 Cor	Titus	Tt	Jude	Jude
Galatians	Gal	Philemon	Phm	Revelation	Rv

Table of Contents

Introduction to the Easter Season

FOREWORD

The story of Karen and her children can illustrate the joy, peace, and hope of the Easter season. When Karen found out that another baby was on the way, she did what she could to prepare her three-year-old son Michael for a new sibling. They found out that the new baby was going to be a girl, and day after day, evening after evening, Michael sang to his sister in Mommy's tummy a song he especially liked: "You are my sunshine, my only sunshine...."

The pregnancy progressed normally for Karen. Then the labor pains came. But complications arose during delivery. There were hours of labor. Finally, Michael's little sister was born. But she was in serious condition. With its siren howling in the night, the ambulance rushed the infant to the neonatal intensive care unit at a special hospital.

The days inched by. The little girl was getting worse. The pediatric specialist told the parents, "There's very little hope. Be prepared for the worst." Karen and her husband contacted a cemetery about a burial plot. Michael kept begging his parents to let him see his sister. "I want to sing to her," he said.

However, children weren't allowed in the Intensive Care Unit. But Karen made up her mind that if Michael didn't see his sister now, he might never see her alive. She dressed him in an oversized scrub suit and marched him into ICU. He looked like a walking laundry basket. The head nurse bellowed, "Get that kid out of here! No children are allowed!" The usually mild-mannered Karen glared steel-eyed into the head nurse's face, her lips a firm line. "He's not leaving until he sings to his sister!"

Karen towed Michael to his sister's bedside. He gazed at the tiny infant losing her battle to live. And he began to sing. In the pure-hearted voice of a three-year-old, Michael sang: "You are my sunshine, my only sunshine, you make me happy when skies are gray...." Instantly the baby girl responded. Her pulse rate became calm and steady.

Michael kept on singing: "You'll never know, dear, how much I love you. Please don't take my sunshine away...." The baby's ragged, strained breathing became smooth.

Michael continued to sing: "The other night, dear, as I lay sleeping, I dreamed I held you in my arms...." Michael's little sister relaxed as rest — healing rest — seemed to sweep over her. Tears conquered the face of the bossy head nurse. Karen glowed.

Michael sang: "You are my sunshine, my only sunshine. Please don't take my sunshine away."

The next day — the very next day — the little girl was well enough to go home! Funeral plans were scrapped. The medical staff called it a miracle. Karen called it a revelation of God's love and the persistence of hope.

The story of God's relations with the human race has both sadness and joy. The New Testament repeatedly relates, for example, the sad account of Jesus' death. The Christian Church insisted that Jesus had truly died, perhaps to counter various movements that wanted to view Jesus' death as a trance, sleep, or some mere appearance so as to avoid the scandalous idea of God becoming fully human and mortal.

But there's also Jesus' *Resurrection*. This celebrates something special never known before or since. It's so far beyond any human concept, and so much solely God's plan, that people have had a hard time trying to comprehend it. It's not *resuscitation*, which is a revival from apparent death or unconsciousness. It's not *metempsychosis*, a theory of some ancients like Plato and Pythagoras that posited the passing of a soul at death into another body, either human or animal. Nor is it *reincarnation*, a rebirth after death in new forms of life. This last is a favorite of some Eastern religions like Hinduism and Buddhism and of theosophy and spiritualism, which make the new life either higher or lower in form depending on one's previous life, until full purification is attained.

Our belief in Jesus' Resurrection celebrates our own resurrection, too. In our Nicene Creed we affirm: "I believe in the resurrection of the body and life everlasting." The essential unity of the human person, who is created as a totality in the image of God, involves immortality of both soul and body. Our resurrection is the reintegration of the person — body and soul — on the last day.

For all who follow Christ, the Easter season, stretching from Easter Sunday to Pentecost, is "party time." Our Easter party is a time of stimulated consciousness, an invitation to penetrate more deeply, to enjoy, enjoy, enjoy.

Easter is a season of "alleluia." The untranslatable "alleluia" is a compound word of joy derived from *hallel* (to praise), the suffix *u* (denoting the second person plural), and *Jah* (the abbreviated form of *Jahvé,* God). In the New Testament, the word is used only in the vision of the worship of God in the Book of Revelation (19:1, 3f., 6). It's sung repeatedly in the Easter season, when it's especially joyous.

A society that applauds war, a society that willingly executes its offenders, a society that has lost interest in the rehabilitation of its imprisoned, a society that's a culture of death, doesn't seem to understand Easter. That's because it doesn't believe in the dignity of the human person, conversion, repentance, or renewal of life. The Easter symbols of new life — colored eggs, flowers newly bloomed, baby chicks — are there, but the substance is missing.

When Michelangelo was doing his famous frescoes in the Vatican's Sistine Chapel, he is alleged to have remarked to his fellow painters: "Why do you keep filling gallery after gallery with endless pictures of the one ever-reiterated theme of Christ in weakness, of Christ upon the cross, Christ dying, Christ hanging dead? Why do you stop there as if the curtain closed upon that horror? Keep the curtain open, and with the cross in the foreground, let us see beyond it to the Easter dawn with the beams streaming upon the risen Christ, Christ alive, Christ ruling, Christ triumphant. For we should be ringing out over the world that Christ has won, that evil is toppling, that the end is sure, and that death is followed by victory. That is... the trumpet blast to... send us... happily upon our way, laughing and singing and recklessly unafraid, because the feel of victory is in the air, and our hearts thrill to it."

For centuries joyful Christians were known as "Easter people," and Easter was the principal festival on the Church calendar. The central theme of the Easter cycle — the death and Resurrection of Christ — is not merely an historical commemoration, but a here-and-now manifestation in the Christian assembly of Jesus' glorification, and a fervent prayer for full realization of the redemption of humankind brought about by Jesus. Like the Jewish Pasch, Easter celebrates deliverance from slavery: in this case the slavery of sin and death. Early on, this rich theme began to incorporate others. Easter is the ideal time for the initiation of new members into the community of the saved and for their acceptance into the Body of Christ by Baptism, Confirmation, and first Eucharist.

In contrast with the Lenten themes of renewal, fasting, penance, and prayer, the Easter season developed into more joyful themes associated with the appearances of the risen Christ to his disciples, his Ascension into heaven, and the sending of the Holy Spirit. The Easter season was a transformation of the Jewish celebration between their Passover and their Pentecost, during which they joyfully commemorated their possession of the promised land.

The Easter prefaces demonstrate the season's themes: the

true lamb took away the sins of the world; dying he destroyed our death, rising he restored our life; we have new life in Christ; Jesus made us children of the light; Jesus gave new and everlasting life; Jesus' death is our ransom from death, his Resurrection our rising to life; the joy of the Resurrection renews the whole world; Jesus lives and intercedes for us forever; we have greater joy than ever in this Easter season; Jesus the victim dies no more; a new age has dawned; the long reign of sin is ended; a broken world has been renewed; people are once again made whole; Jesus' perfect sacrifice fulfilled all others; Jesus has opened the gates of heaven; Jesus is our ransom from death; he's our rising to life; Jesus pleads our cause; Jesus' Resurrection accomplished the restoration of the universe.

SCRIPTURE READINGS IN THE EASTER CYCLE

Portions of St. Luke's second New Testament book, the Acts of the Apostles, constitute the usual first readings for the Masses of the Easter season. The book treats that vital period in Christian history between the Resurrection of Jesus and the death of St. Paul. This was the time when Christian beliefs were being crystallized and the organization of the Church into a world-wide movement was being developed.

The term "Acts of the Apostles" is a misnomer, because it has little to say concerning most of the original Twelve. The activities of St. Peter are described at some length and mention is made of St. John and St. Philip, but more than half of the book is about St. Paul. The first section reports several sermons containing essential Christian beliefs.

The beautiful Gospel of St. John is the other major New Testament work in the Easter liturgies. John's symbol is the eagle, because his Gospel begins with the preexistence of Jesus in heaven and expresses thoughts that soar.

Containing many details about Jesus not found in the other Gospels, John's narration begins with the Word of God becoming a human being in Jesus. Jesus is also God. Because his will is in complete harmony with the Father's will, it's proper to refer to him as the Son of God and to understand John's statement that, to as many as believed in him, he gave the power to become children of God.

Jesus' authenticity was witnessed by God Himself. As we see in our meditation for Monday of the Sixth Week of Easter, other witnesses were John the Baptist, the ancient Scriptures, Jesus' followers, and Jesus' own life-giving words and signs. Yet Jesus was rejected by that aspect of the world that was condemnable, especially the leaders of his own people. He died as a sacrifice of love to bring light and life into the darkness and blindness of the world. His Resurrection, which we so joyfully celebrate in this season, is another witness to his victory.

The purpose of John's Gospel, as stated by the author, was to show that Jesus of Nazareth was the Christ, the Son of God, and that by believing in him we might have eternal life. This Gospel narrative has been organized and adapted to serve the evangelist's theological purposes. Among these are opposition to the synagogue and to those followers of John the Baptist who tried to exalt their master at Jesus' expense, a wish to show that Jesus is the Messiah, and a desire to convince Christians that their religious belief and practice must be rooted in Jesus.

The central theme is the divine *Logos*, the Word which was with God and which was God. Jesus' miracles were accomplished by virtue of the power of God. John calls these miracles "signs," and uses each of them as a kind of introduction to a discourse containing Jesus' message.

John records only seven of these "signs," in contrast with the many more which are reported in the synoptic Gospels. These seven are the turning of water into wine at the marriage feast in Cana, the healing of the nobleman's son, the healing of the man at the sheep-gate pool, walking on water, the feeding of five thousand people, the healing of the man born blind, and the raising of Lazarus from death. In the case of Lazarus, which is the climax, John shows its deeper meaning with Jesus' statement, "I am the Resurrection and the life...."

John's Gospel also records incidents that are closely related to the closing days of Jesus' ministry. The major emphasis in this part is to be found in Jesus' discourses. Here John is interpreting the meaning of Jesus' earthly career from the perspective of the post-Resurrection experiences and beliefs of the Christian community.

The author — whether the disciple John, or one of his followers, or someone under the disciple's guidance — was an artistic and theological genius who used his Gospel to respond to the pressing theological needs of his time. Throughout Christian history, this Gospel has been read and cherished far more than any of the other accounts of Jesus. Its language is simple enough to be read and appreciated by the uneducated, and yet is so profound that it appeals to the most highly educated.

SOME DISTINCTIVE TRAITS OF THE EASTER SEASON

The Easter season emphasizes many upbeat Christian trademark themes. Notable among them are joy, peace, and hope.

Joy

In our meditation for Thursday of the Fifth Week of Easter we see that there are several terms similar to joy: happiness, beatitude, pleasure, delight. *Joy* is the preferred term when the happiness is at its most intense. Jesus' new and peerless joy that can come our way is more fulfilling than any other and with a new completeness. A joyless Christian is a contradiction in terms.

Laughter in the Bible goes all the way back to the Book of Genesis. There it is recorded that three men, appearing before Abraham, prophesied that within one year his wife Sarah would have a son. She, eavesdropping, heard, and Genesis tells us (18:12) that she laughed to herself and asked, "Now that I am so withered and my husband is so old, am I still to have sexual pleasure?"

The story gets funnier. After God asked Abraham why Sarah laughed, Sarah, because she was afraid, dissembled, saying, "I didn't laugh." But God said, "Yes, you did" (v. 15). Then Abraham laughed as he said to himself, "Can a child be born to a man who is a hundred years old? Or can Sarah give birth at ninety?" (v. 17). Born of their union was Isaac, whose name means "laughter." After his birth, Sarah said, "God has given me cause to laugh, and all who hear of it will laugh with me" (Gn 21:6).

The Jewish Scriptures are full of other references to one or another aspect of joy. The Law of Moses mandated that we rejoice before the Lord our God in all that we undertake (Dt 12:18). The Psalmist tells us that "He who is throned in heaven laughs" (Ps 2:4). The Book of Proverbs, an encapsulation of practical wisdom, said that "a glad heart makes a cheerful countenance" (15:13) and noted that, whereas it's slow death to be gloomy all the time, being cheerful keeps you healthy (17:22). Proverbs also says that the ideal wife "is clothed with strength and dignity, and laughs at the days to come" (Pr 31:25).

The author of Job motivates with the promise that God "will fill your mouth with laughter and your lips with rejoicing" (Jb 8:21). Sirach, telling us how to recognize a true wise man, tells us that "a man's attire, his hearty laughter, and his gait proclaim him for what he is" (Si 19:26).

Although the Gospels don't record any instance of Jesus laughing outright, there *are* instances of his humor; it would be most surprising if he didn't enjoy, for instance, the wedding reception at Cana. All the expressions in the Jewish Scriptures about joy and laughter were, after all, his tradition. The result of following his advice, says Jesus, will be joy (Jn 15:11, Thursday, Fifth Week of Easter). It's *his unique* joy. On the very eve of his crucifixion, Jesus astonished his disciples by telling them that he'd been speaking to them that his joy may be in them and their joy may be complete (Jn 15:11).

Jesus' Resurrection helps us to understand that intense pleasure and joy. The empty tomb is the very image of that unbreakable human aspiration for joy, exactly as God understands it. Jesus' Resurrection is the supreme affirmation that at the end of life joy, not suffering, has the last word.

St. Paul's letters, too, are full of joy. And St. James wrote that we should consider it all joy when we encounter various trials (Jm 1:2). St. Peter observed that "although you have not seen Jesus you love him, and you rejoice with an indescribable and glorious joy" (1 P 1:8). And in two of his letters, St. John wrote that he was writing that our joy may be complete (1 Jn 1:4; 2 Jn 1:12).

Our meditation for Friday of the Sixth Week of Easter opines that we Christians evangelize and sanctify suffering, but we don't sufficiently evangelize joy. In today's world, to evangelize pleasure and joy is no less important than to evangelize pain. Youth — and not only they — are erroneously led to think of God as an enemy of joy, that every explosion of joy is a sin.

The Christian tradition — even with a cross as its central symbol — continues the principle of joy. Many of the sayings of the early monks who were known as the Desert Fathers were renowned for their humor. St. Bernard of Clairvaux called their sayings, said with a smile or with tongue in cheek, *jucunda* ("a playful devotion"), a Latin word from which the English word "joke" derives.

In an Easter sermon, Saint John Chrysostom described a vision of Christ confronting the devil and laughing at him. St. Francis of Assisi said such things as, "I am God's clown; men come to me and laugh at me, and I laugh with them.… Spiritual joy fills our hearts.… Be joyful in the Lord and be merry.… Go out happy, joyful, and praising God." St. Thomas Aquinas, knowing that sadness is a thing of the devil and an enemy of the spiritual life, proposed as a cure a good sleep and a bath. St. Thomas More said, "It is possible to live for the next life and be merry in this."

Even Martin Luther said: "God is not a God of sadness, but the devil is.… A Christian should and must be a cheerful person." Said John Wesley: "Sour godliness is the devil's religion." John Calvin, too, laughed: "We are nowhere forbidden to laugh, or to be satisfied with food… or to be delighted with music, or to drink wine." And a relatively modern wise man, G.K. Chesterton, said, "Like water does for the body, laughter does for the soul."

This serene and joyful attitude to life, the *gaudium cum pace* ("joy with peace," *Roman Missal*, Preparation for Mass; cf. Thursday, Fifth Week of Easter) doesn't mean the absence of difficulties. Jesus wants his Apostles to have peace even in and with his departure. In fact, even in the face of his forthcoming departure, Jesus said, "If you loved me, you would rejoice" (Jn 14:28). Joy has to be pursued and conquered by a struggle against our evil tendencies, which are constant. Our religion teaches us penance as a means; joy is its aim.

Joy is one of the most irresistible powers in the world: It brings about calm, it soothes away anger. Norman Cousins found watching comedies a help against the pain of cancer. What's more, a joyful countenance attracts people to God, showing them what the presence of God produces within the soul.

Joy expresses itself in *laughter*, *dancing*, and *humor*.

Laughter is a need of all time. The exercise value of laughter is so great that one physician claimed that laughing 100 times a day is the equivalent of 10 minutes of strenuous rowing.

Laughter lightens a heavy heart. Laughter in the face of

tribulation doesn't always indicate an attempt to deny, belittle, or cover up the pain. Rather, the laughter says, "Yes, it hurts, but humor helps remind me that this pain is only temporary."

Laughter gets the job done. Thomas Carlyle wrote: "The cheerful person will do more in the same time, will do it better, will persevere in it longer, than the sad or sullen person." And Michel de Montaigne said, "The plainest sign of wisdom is a continual cheerfulness."

Dancing, too, is an instinctive activity of the joy of the Judeo-Christian tradition. After Pharaoh's horses and chariots and charioteers had drowned during the Jews' Exodus from Egypt, "Miriam, Aaron's sister, went out with all the women with tambourines, dancing" (Ex 15:20). On David's return after slaying Goliath, "women came out from each of the cities of Israel to meet Saul and David, singing and dancing, with tambourines and joyful songs" (1 S 18:6).

When the Israelites were bringing the Ark of the Covenant to Jerusalem, David "came before the Lord dancing with abandon" (2 S 6:14). Even the somber Jeremiah, presenting prophecies about the future of Jerusalem during bad times, promised the people that they "shall go forth dancing with the merrymakers" (31:4) and that "the virgins shall make merry and dance, and young men and old as well" (31:13). Although we have no instance of the Gospels explicitly saying that Jesus danced, he could have danced at the wedding reception at Cana.

Humor, like laughter, is a resurrection. Both allow us to rise again and again. People with a sense of humor encourage others to be optimistic in times of trial by pointing out the bright side of a situation. Humor can play an important role in preventing natural feelings of grief and sadness from becoming larger than the event itself. Important for Christians are the sentiments expressed by Blessed Julian of Norwich, who wrote: "The greatest honor you can give to Almighty God is to live gladly, joyfully, because of the knowledge of His love."

One of the most joyous of the post-Resurrection accounts of meetings with the risen Jesus is told by St. Luke (24:13-25; see Wednesday of the Octave of Easter). Cleopas and his companion were disciples of Jesus — not Apostles or intimate friends, but followers. This may help to explain why they didn't recognize Jesus. They'd left Jerusalem downcast because of their disappointment that Jesus their hope had been crucified — the end of their dream, they thought.

Jesus set them straight and gave them joy by instructing them that his death — and Resurrection — was in fulfillment of the Scriptures. Although Luke in his Gospel doesn't tell us precisely what Jesus said, an educated guess tells us that what Jesus spoke of was the constant scriptural theme that's also the theme of the Easter season and of this book: that God reveals Himself unceasingly as the One whose characteristic work is to bring life out of death, joy out of sorrow.

Peace

Another gift which we specially celebrate during the Easter season is peace. Peace — external and internal — is vital for all of us. Problems of internal peace such as undue anxiety and scrupulosity we consider all the time. We commemorate external peace at special times like Memorial Day.

Jesus made peace an important part of his last lessons the night before he died. He said that he was giving us *his* gift of peace, "not as the world gives" (Jn 14:27-31; Tuesday, Fifth Week of Easter).

Usually a going-away gift is for the person who is leaving. Jesus reversed that procedure and gave his disciples his farewell gift of peace at his going away. Strangely, he said he was telling them of his forthcoming suffering and death so that they might have peace in him (Jn 16:33; Monday, Seventh Week of Easter). His peace was the *shalom* of ancient Israel, the Arabic *salaam*.

These beautiful words are untranslatable, but peace is their dominant characteristic — and harmony, well-being in every sense, and prosperity.

The key to this peace is found in Jesus' phrase that we're to have peace "in me" (Jn 16:33; see Monday of the Seventh Week of Easter). He commands/invites us to abide in him (Jn 15:4; see Wednesday of the Fifth Week). Now, the place where we "abide" is where we're at home. Home, in its best sense, is where we're nourished, where we come to know ourselves and one another, where we love and are loved, where we're shaped into whom we're to become. God's powerfully transforming love lives among us and through us in the peace of the risen Christ. In that kind of life, our heavenly Father is glorified (Jn 15:8).

What the world means by "peace" is often simply the absence of war. By the Tiber River in Rome there is a glass-enclosed beautifully-carved marble *ara pacis,* "altar of peace." It was erected by Augustus Caesar after he and his armies had conquered practically all of Europe and the known parts of Asia. But when one bends others to one's will, that's not peace, but tyranny (see Tuesday of the Fifth Week of Easter).

Or the world's peace is a state of being left alone, like what the harassed mother wants from her active young children or the worker from the public he has had to deal with for too long. Or it's not being burdened by cares or financial worries. Or it's a deep sleep, which is what the world often understands when it writes "Rest in Peace" on its tombstones.

What Jesus means by peace — God's gift — he gave us especially through his Resurrection. God's peace is loving communion with Him, with one's neighbor, and with oneself. Jesus had God's peace as he fulfilled his mission, even on the way of the cross. It's the kind of peace that St. Maximilian Kolbe had when in the Nazi concentration camp he gave his life to save another inmate: intended to be starved to death, that was too slow for his killers, who injected him to hasten the process. It's the kind of peace that the Japanese martyrs in Nagasaki had when they sang hymns of praise to God as they were being crucified. It's the kind of peace that the Ugandan martyrs had when they were being burned to death.

Peace is an *active* thing: a virtue, a state of mind, a disposition for benevolence. It contains certain prerequisites. If you want peace, you must have a still and quiet conscience, because there's no peace for the wicked (Is 48:22). If you want peace, you must work for justice: violent injustices in society create a breeding ground for interpersonal violence. The combination of aggression, depression, stress, anxiety, and uncertainty that results from wickedness gives birth to the anger that serves as the perfect breeding ground for hate crimes and other forms of interpersonal mayhem. Societally, these can lead to war.

If you want peace, you must seek God's will. In Gethsemane Jesus prayed that, if it be the heavenly Father's will, he be spared the coming suffering and crucifixion; he wasn't spared, but was granted the Resurrection instead. As Dante put over the doors of paradise, "In His will is our peace." T.S. Eliot observed that if we do God's will we can find peace "even among these rocks" of our life. Jesus said that one of the essential requirements of peace is love; in our often brutal world, that can summon what we today call "tough love."

Only when we truly find our life in the Risen One can we understand Jesus' otherwise absurd claim to have conquered the world (Jn 16:33; see Monday of the Seventh Week). Jesus recalled that reality on the eve of his death. The literal meaning of the Greek word that followed (*tharseite*), translated "take courage," is to have confidence and firmness of purpose in the face of danger. His "peace," then, is the state of being that flows directly from this confidence and firmness of purpose. Fortified with this living in the Risen One, we know in the depths of our being a peace that the world can neither give nor take away.

His kind of peace is a way of his saying, "I'm giving eternal life." Jesus' "eternal life" stresses not the duration of life, but its quality. It's the highest life possible: the life of God Himself in us. It surrounds and infuses every aspect of our life with peace: peace with people because we're all God's children, peace with life itself because we live in a friendly universe, and peace with ourselves because of a new insight into and humble acceptance of our weaknesses.

We're to be peace-makers, peace-givers. Those are the highest callings within civilization. We must be free of discouragement, impatience, and anger at failure in our efforts for peace, and be sincere, humble, and wise in seeking it. In our daily lives we must reflect nonviolence as a positive force. Let's repeat constantly the beautiful words Jesus advised: "Peace be to this household" (Lk 10:5). Peace is our greeting, and peace is our mark. Peace is one of the signs of the presence of the kingdom. Reducing conflict and violence — not only at the international level but also in our homes, offices, churches, and communities — is a priority. War can't resolve our differences. Nonviolence — skills and tools to engage in the dialogue — is the way to diminish conflict.

Jesus' subversive idea is that, if the world wants peace, the wolves in whose midst he sent his followers like lambs (Lk 10:3) must swap power for trust, manipulation for solidarity, greed for sharing. That isn't a world that the wolves of war and violence can survive in. It makes them very angry, and vicious in their attack.

Jesus tells us through his emissaries that the kingdom of God "is at hand for you" (Lk 10:9). It's "at hand" and "for you." It's not up in the sky or across the sea, but right here with us whenever and wherever we want to call upon it. With our cooperation, God's power can transform *this* world, with all its problems, into a place of peace and justice.

Peace isn't a given; it has to be continually worked for and worked at. The search for peace must begin with *individuals*, then radiate out — to family, community, nation, and world. In that process, we recognize the truth of the Chinese saying that "the first step is the longest." If you haven't found Jesus' deep peace, take the first step — the long one — of praying for a heart to welcome it.

The Church continues the risen Jesus' ideals of peace. She sees peace as St. Augustine's "tranquility of order"; it's the work of justice and the effect of charity (*Catechism of the Catholic Church*, #2304). The Church looks upon both justice and peace as having a faith dimension, sees both as scripturally based, and has said much about peace. Vatican Council II, for example, said that "the Church… consolidates peace among men for the glory of God" (*Gaudium et Spes*, 76). The Council also voiced the wish that those who are involved in the work of education and the people who mold public opinion "should regard it as their most important task to educate the minds of men to renewed sentiments of peace" (*Ibid.*, 82). The Church has, whenever acceptable, been connected with the furtherance of peace, very often through papal pronouncements and involvement.

An anonymous poet has said, not without great truth: "Give me the money that's been spent in war and I will clothe every man, woman, and child in the attire of which kings and queens would be proud. I will build a schoolhouse in every valley over the earth. I will crown every hillside with a place of worship consecrated to the Gospel of peace."

Less poetically, think of the real-life possibilities of a country not having to support a military establishment: a better standard of living; a high percent of its national budget for health; a high literacy rate; choice education free at all levels; well-stocked public libraries; theaters and symphony orchestras that are state-subsidized but not state-controlled; a public transport system that's cheap, clean, and punctual; paved roads that are a dream, with scarcely a pothole; many national parks; and a well-funded ecology program that could become a mecca for bird-watchers and provide clean air and safe water.

Hope

The Resurrection of our Lord gives hope to those who struggle for it. Through his Resurrection Jesus snatched victory from the jaws of defeat, vindicated his life and teachings, and confirmed having faith in him. It's the most exciting event of world history. It isn't only an event that happened once in the past; it's the power of God that's seen constantly in people's inner experience of the newness of life. All that we do at Easter shows our joy and our hope: in church, flowers, white vestments, and joyous music; elsewhere, coloring Easter eggs, wearing nice clothes, dining together. All other Sundays are "little Easters."

Hope isn't optimism. Optimism usually implies a temperamental confidence that all will turn out for the best, often suggesting a failure to consider things closely. Hope means treating the future as really future — that is, unknowable — and treating the present as really present — that is, inescapable.

Scriptural hope is much more than "thinking positive thoughts." It doesn't promise that our projects will succeed or that we will find within ourselves the capacity to overcome all obstacles. Biblical hope is bluntly realistic. Its roots in Scripture are full of stories about evil, sin, domination, war, pain, and failure. It meets these with a relentless insistence that God is bringing a new creation to birth. Despite discouragement, hurt, and exhaustion, and despite our limitations and the smallness of our efforts, God is at work in our lives and in the world.

The optimism of an abundantly cheerful temperament enables a person to see people, events, and situations "through rose-colored spectacles" — that is, in their most attractive and alluring aspects. It implies illusion or delusion. Hope, on the other hand, usually implies some ground, often reasonably good ground, for one's looking up. It therefore typically, but not invariably, suggests confidence, in which there's no self-deception and which is the result of a realistic consideration of the possibilities. Whereas optimism is the belief that things are going to get better, hope is the belief that together we can *make* them better. Hope makes death bearable. Hope is the mainstay of our energy.

There's nothing wrong with optimism, but the theological virtue of hope is much more. Hope is, ultimately, a gift from God given to sustain us during difficult times. Hope is the little child that walks between the adults of faith and love. When the adults grow tired, the little one instills new life and energy. Hope never allows our faith to grow weak or our love to falter.

Realism without hope may easily lead to a kind of self-defeating cynicism, bitterness, and despair. On the other hand hope without realism may lead to a kind of ivory tower daydreaming. To combine them is the enormous task: to keep our head in the stars but our feet firmly planted on the earth. St. Augustine said, "Hope has two daughters — anger and courage. Anger at the way things are, and courage to work to make things other than they are." That can lead to transformation. And transformation is a marvelous thing.

Hope began with Jesus' very birth. The Christmas carol sums it up: "The hopes and fears / of *all* the years / are met in thee tonight!" Jesus' speech and actions throughout his life, too, looked to his Resurrection and the hope that it generated. Matthew spoke of Jesus (Mt 12:21) as the fulfillment of the words of Isaiah that the Gentiles would hope in his name (Is 42:4). And Jesus gave hope to us all when he declared that he'd come to call not the righteous, but sinners (Lk 5:32). Of all Jesus' actions, his Resurrection is the cornerstone of our hope.

Peter and Judas present lessons in hope. Peter was guilty of denial that was tantamount to betrayal, and Judas of actual betrayal. Peter had an attitude of trust and hope; ultimately, he gave his life for Jesus. Judas, on the other hand, had an attitude of distrust and despair, fled from the compassionate Jesus, and hung himself.

Christian hope is continued in St. Paul's epistles. Like Jesus' deceptively simple parables, Paul reminded the Romans (Rm 8:18-25) that there's a much wider vision of life than is comprehended at first sight. The glory which the believer is destined to share with Christ far exceeds the sufferings of the present life, which is only a transition to the assured glory that awaits us in the end.

We can say, along with Paul in his Letter to the Romans (8:25), that we hope for what we don't see and we wait for it with patience. Paul outlines everything he had hoped for under the Jewish law: freedom, knowing how to please God, God's presence, new life, becoming a true child of God, the hope of glory, and the knowledge that everything would work out for good.

Paul finds the fulfillment of all his hopes in the continual intercession of the risen Christ (v. 34). Nothing will separate us from Christ's love for us (v. 35). Looking into the future, not even another world can take away our being enveloped in the love of God if we don't let it. The love of God manifested in the Christ-event is the unshakable basis of Christian life and hope.

Paul's letter, filled with hope, encouragement, and expectation, intertwines the cosmic vision of Isaiah and the everyday life of the Christian. Paul tells us (8:24f.) it's through our hope in the redemption of our bodies that we're saved. Further, a hope that can be seen, he reminds us, isn't truly a hope: Who hopes for what they can already see?

The doctrine of Jesus' Resurrection finds its most sublime expression in the fifteenth chapter of Paul's First Letter to the Corinthians.

First, Paul proves the resurrection of our body (vv. 1-19) from Christ's Resurrection. Christ appeared to many in his risen body: to Peter, to the Apostles, to more than five hundred people, to James — and, eventually, also to Paul himself. If Christ hasn't risen, there's no hope: Paul's preaching, and our faith, are empty, not resting on any reality (v. 14). Christ is the first-fruit of those who have died.

Second, he proves the resurrection of our body (vv. 20-25) from the efficacy of Christ's redemption: as death came through one man, Adam, so by one man, Christ, comes resurrection of the dead. At the end, Christ will deliver the kingdom to God the Father. The last enemy to be destroyed will be death.

Third, Paul argues to our resurrection from practical faith: the life and customs of the faithful (vv. 29-34). If the dead don't rise, let's live by the principle to eat and drink, for tomorrow we die (v. 32). This principle was enunciated in the Book of Ecclesiastes (8:15), where it meant the table as the place of refreshment as well as relaxation: a connotation of well-being, prosperity, and happiness — the full range of life's blessings.

Fourth, Paul argues to our resurrection from a comparison with a seed (vv. 35-44). A seed isn't brought to life unless it dies. In our case, the natural body that's sown gives rise to a spiritual body.

Fifth, Paul argues from Christ's full victory over death (vv. 26, 54-57): the sting of death is swallowed up in Jesus' victory.

In his Second Letter to the Corinthians (5:6-10), Paul catalogues his apostolic trials and afflictions, but the negative never completely prevails; there's always some experience of rescue, of hope, of salvation. Paul's sufferings are connected with Christ's, and his deliverance is a sign that he's to share in Christ's Resurrection.

When Paul wrote his Letter to the Colossians right after the middle of the first century, conditions for the Christian religion were at least as bad as anything today. Paul taught that Jesus alone is exalted above all creation. We're to live where Christ is — not only individually, but as a community: We're a risen community, we're an Easter people, and "alleluia" is our song. Through baptism, we died with Christ and shared his new and risen life of the first Easter (3:3).

In his First Letter to the Thessalonians (1:1-5), Paul picks out the three essential responses of people to the Gospel: their "work of *faith*", their "labor of *love*" (*agape*), and their patient endurance of suffering "in *hope*" — hope of the Lord's second coming. We can endure a lot if we have hope, because then we're walking toward the dawn.

The object of Christian hope is specific: Jesus died and rose (4:14). True Christians look upon the *leitmotif* of death that courses through our lives not as a dreadful end to everything, or solely as a time of judgment, but as a participation in Jesus' death and Resurrection and as our last act of giving to our heavenly Father.

Paul's Letter to the Ephesians asserts (1:17-23) that Jesus' Resurrection and Ascension overcame the sins that put him to death (v. 20). The Resurrection and Ascension and glorification of Jesus, taken as one great continuous act of the Father, is to Paul the supreme proof of the power of God. That power brought into stark relief the contrasts between the despair and darkness before that great event and the hope and light after it.

There are other New Testament statements pertinent to hope. The Letter to the Hebrews (6:19) tells us that hope is the steadfast anchor of the soul. The First Letter of Peter is one of the more important letters to the group of Christians who were suffering severe persecution at the hands of the Roman government. Our life, says that letter, is patterned, in an unbelieving world, on the death and Resurrection of Jesus. God's saving action begins in a big way with new birth through baptism. Our new birth is a birth to many things, among them a birth to *hope* (1:3), a hope which draws its life from what happened to Jesus in his rising from the dead. As we view our hope, our inheritance, and our salvation — our eternal life bestowed in baptism — there's cause for rejoicing (v. 6).

The Letter of James (5:9-12) tells us that in our pursuit of friendships we must, in particular, be patient — with a special kind of patience. What's desirable is a patience that doesn't lose hope, no matter how hard the situation; a patience that's strong and at the same time gentle; a patience that's not supine, but active. It's a patience that's a quiet, everyday sort of strength. Christian patience is based on a conviction of divine mercy and the hope of the coming of the Lord (v. 11).

The Church upholds Christian allegiance to hope. Early on, when the Church was being persecuted, she used the anchor as a sign of hope in Christ. The Church's liturgy continues with hope. We pray before Communion at Mass, "Protect us from all anxiety as we wait *in joyful hope* for the coming of our Savior, Jesus Christ." It's a special kind of waiting for Jesus the savior, the Christ, the only Son of God, the Lord (*Catechism of the Catholic Church*, #430-451). The final petition of the Eucharistic Prayer is, "We hope to enjoy forever the vision of your glory."

Of the three theological virtues of faith, hope, and charity, hope has tended to become rather neglected. We pay attention to faith because much of religious education is concerned with what we believe. We learn that love is the virtue which sums up all of the other virtues, so we see its importance.

But we must have hope. Some people in Kenya say that a dog in the water that sees the shore doesn't drown. Everyone in difficulty has to see the shore. In the midst of our many wake-up calls — accidents, illnesses, deaths of people close to us — we're to be people of vision, of hope, of eternity. As the flippant T-shirt label put it: "Life Is Uncertain — Eat Dessert First."

Today, the real challenge is not only to believe in Jesus' Resurrection — the facts are there — but to discover the energy that the early disciples found through it. Jesus' Resurrection tells us that in Jesus we find God's power to save us. We have to accept the challenge of working to forge Jesus' message of life and hope for our world. That entails involvement with the affairs of the world. The hope of heaven doesn't weaken commitment to the progress of the earthly city, but rather gives it meaning and strength.

Living without hope is no longer living. One of the world's masterpieces of literature is Dante's *The Divine Comedy*. In it the poet takes a personal journey through hell, purgatory, and heaven. Since hell can be defined as life without hope, it's no accident that the poet sees at the entrance to hell the words: "Abandon all hope, you who enter here." In the midst of difficulty and hard times, we persevere in hope. Man's way leads to a hopeless end; God's way leads to an endless hope!

If we sense that someone has great hope in us, we're buoyed up, and we feel that we can soar. Whenever we hope in people, we make their burden light. Such hope in people has its risks. In marriage a man and a woman pledge their love with hope in one another, yet they add the risk that they willingly accept: "for better or *for worse*, for richer or *for poorer, in sickness* and in health." Hope has high stakes and risks everything for a future that remains unknown. We live by faith, are renewed in love, and walk in hope.

AFTERWORD

A minister, a priest, and a rabbi were on a workshop panel at an ecumenical conference. Somebody in the audience asked them, "If you were suddenly to fall over dead on the street, how would you want to be remembered?"

The minister replied, "I would want people to say, 'he was truly born again, and lived out the social gospel.'"

The priest replied, "I would want to people to say, 'he faithfully administered the sacraments and reached out to the poor.'"

The rabbi pondered the question and replied, "I would want people to say, 'Wait — he's moving!'"

But death is a reality. Only Jesus has overcome it. What would have been the history of Christianity, or of the world for that matter, if Jesus had merely been put to death and not raised?

He might well have gone down as a great spiritual leader like Socrates or Gandhi, but hardly the focal point for a new religion. Both the ancient Jews and cultured pagans had questions about whether the distant "God in Heaven" *really cared* about what happened to humans. The revolutionary idea of a human being who was also God rising from death resolved doubts about God's concern in a radical way.

Consider the impact of Jesus' Resurrection on the average person. Suddenly death needn't mean "the end," but the beginning of something new — not just for rulers, philosophers, and heroes, whom theretofore people thought might stand some chance of immortality, but even for the lowest slave!

The Resurrection of Jesus was the most momentous occasion since the crisp newness of the initial days of creation. Think of the wonder of the initial creation. Among the theories about how we got here, what we now think we know is this. About 4.6 billion years ago a great swirl of gas and dust some 15 billion miles across accumulated in space where we are now and began to aggregate. Virtually all of it — 99.9% of the mass of the solar system — went to make the sun. Out of the floating material that was left over, two microscopic grains floated close enough together to be joined by electrostatic forces. This was the moment of conception for our planet Earth. In about 300 thousand years, the Earth was essentially formed.

Over and against that wonder of the initial creation, the Resurrection of Jesus brought about a new, even more wonderful creation. Jesus' Resurrection was so unique that, when during his life Jesus had spoken of it, the Apostles didn't know what "rising from the dead" meant (Mk 9:10). That's because it represented something unheard-of: the disaster of death had been turned into the triumph of life.

When we say or sing, "Jesus Christ is risen today," we don't mean only "Jesus Christ was risen once upon a time." We mean that the risen Christ is all around us, in the eyes and faces of those sitting beside us, in the bread and wine of the altar, in the newly baptized, in the people we meet all the time. He walks the earth today — teaching, healing, touching, suffering, dying, and rising. If we look for the risen Jesus with faith and hope and love, we will find him. Seek him, find him, love him in every person — by serving their needs. Then truly not only is Christ risen but we, too, are living a risen life by his power and grace.

We Christians don't give in to despair or pessimism, because we believe in God and in him whom God sent. We enjoy life, because we enjoy God. But every generation needs its own shoot springing up from its own tradition, its own breath (*ruach*) of fresh air blowing across the land, its own people who aren't co-opted by the prosperity of the moment. In our pursuit of the joy, peace, and hope of Easter, persistence and determination are more powerful than talent, genius, or education.

A final story makes an important point. Bill had wild hair, wore a T-shirt with holes, jeans, and no shoes. This had been his complete wardrobe for his entire four years of college. He was brilliant and kind of eccentric. He became a Christian while attending college.

Across the street from his campus was a Catholic church. One day Bill decided to go there. He walked in in his usual dress. The Mass had already started. Bill started down the aisle looking for a seat, but the church was completely packed, and he couldn't find a seat. By now, people were looking a bit uncomfortable, but no one said anything.

Bill got closer and closer to the front, and when he realized there were no seats he just squatted down in the aisle. This had never happened in this church before. By now, the people were deadly silent and uptight, the tension in the air thick.

At about this time the priest, approaching the pulpit, realized that from way at the back of the church, the head usher was slowly making his way toward Bill. The silver-haired usher was very dignified. He walked with a cane and, as he started walking toward this young man nothing could be heard but the tap-tap-tap of his cane on the floor.

It seemed to take a terribly long time for the usher to reach the young man. All eyes were focused on the usher. The priest, now in the pulpit, couldn't preach until the usher did what the people thought he had to. When he reached Bill, they saw this elderly man drop his cane on the floor. With great difficulty, he lowered himself and sat down next to the young man so he wouldn't be alone. Everyone choked with emotion.

When the priest gained control, he said, "What I'm about to preach, you will never remember. What you have just seen, you will never forget."

Our lives, not homilies, may be the only Bible some people will ever read.

❧

If in reading these materials you think that the meditations for each day are long, YOU'RE RIGHT! The reason for the length is that we hope you will be able to use a part each year — thus making these materials useful for many years.

If you find these materials helpful and to your liking, you may be happy with my *Pastoral Talks for Special Occasions* (for New Year's Day, Valentine's Day, Graduations, Civil Observances, and so forth); *God Still Speaks: Listen! - Cycle A*, or *All Things Made New - Cycle B*, or *Ode to Joy - Cycle C* (all for Sundays); or *Thirst for Life*, or *The New Out of the Old*, or *Rejoicing in Hope* (all for the weekdays of Ordinary Time), or *Walk in the Light of the Lord* (for the weekdays of the Advent/Christmas Season), or *Embrace Your Renewal* (for the weekdays of Lent) — all published by Alba House, 2187 Victory Blvd., Staten Island, N.Y., 10314; tel. 1-800-343 ALBA (2522).

Ac 2:14, 22-32; Mt 28:8-15

God So Loved the World...

Trial lawyers have a saying: "Drag a few hundred dollars through a money-hungry crowd and you can find plenty of witnesses to testify to whatever you want." This is what happened in today's Gospel. The elders gave the soldiers who guarded Jesus' tomb a large bribe to say that Jesus' disciples came during the night and stole him while they were asleep.

Of course, any good trial lawyer would be able easily to proceed in court against such guards. If the guards were asleep how could they know what was happening? And if they weren't asleep, why didn't they do their guard duty and stop the would-be grave robbers?

It was the first day of the Christian week when the women came to the tomb. No one could visit on the Sabbath, because that would violate the Law of Moses, so by Sunday the women's overpowering love for Jesus could wait no longer. Early in the morning, when it was still dark, they went to the tomb. The risen Jesus came to meet them. They became apostles to the Twelve.

The Gospel frankly admits that the Apostles didn't yet understand the Scripture about Jesus rising from the dead. It wasn't the Scriptures that convinced anyone at the time: it was the empty tomb. In retrospect, one might say that some First Testament passages had suggested the Resurrection (for example, Ps 16:10; Ho 6:2; Jon 1:17; 2:1), and that the Apostles should have understood. But, while it may be true that life may be understood backward, it must be lived forward.

The overpowering wonder of this mystery wasn't intended to paralyze everyone to the point of immobility, nor to stun people beyond words. The Apostles weren't told by the women to build a shrine around the Holy Sepulchre and make it an object of world pilgrimage. They were summoned away from Jerusa-

lem and told to go up north from Judea to Galilee, where they
would see Jesus and receive further instructions about preaching his message.

What we heard in today's reading from St. Luke's Acts of
the Apostles is a masterpiece of condensation of the first recorded
Christian sermon. St. Peter preached it fearlessly on the first
Pentecost, and it's in a nutshell what we believe. According to
Peter's speech, spoken under the inspiration of the Holy Spirit,
all the prophecies and set purposes of God converged upon the
sufferings, death, and Resurrection of Jesus. This doesn't mean
that Jesus' death followed upon some inflexible divine plan. It's
really an attempt to cope with the mystery of why this man could
have been crucified and killed. The answer is: only *God* knows!

And God is, of course, a mystery. A kindergarten teacher
was observing her children while they drew pictures from their
imaginations. She would occasionally walk around to see each
child's art work. She asked one little girl who was working dili-
gently what her drawing was. The girl replied, "I'm drawing God."
The teacher paused and said, "But no one knows what God looks
like." Without missing a beat or looking up from her drawing,
the girl replied, "They will now!"

Peter proclaimed Jesus in the beautiful words of the sixteenth Psalm, which he saw as having foretold Jesus' passion,
death, and Resurrection. The text is given more fully in today's
Responsorial Psalm. In the Psalm's words, God shows us the path
of *life*. His kind of life brings joy.

Joy is never lacking during any part of the Church year,
because it's all connected in one way or another with the Easter
celebration. In these days of the Easter season, though, this joy
particularly shows. By the Lord's crucifixion and Resurrection
we've been saved from eternal death, and Jesus' Resurrection is
the guarantee of our own resurrection.

True joy doesn't depend on mere physical or material well-
being, and isn't diminished by the presence of difficulties. Deep
joy originates in the love that God has shown for us and in our

correspondence with that love. We recognize the Lord's promise that he will give us a joy which no one can take from us (Jn 16:22). Nor can pain take it away, nor calumny, nor abandonment — nor even falls into sin, if we return promptly to the Lord.

Sadness is born of keeping distant from God. When we're sad, we cause damage to others. Sadness debilitates us. It's like the heavy clay accumulating on our shoes if we walk in the rain: it makes each step more difficult.

To be happy is a form of giving thanks to God for the innumerable gifts He gives us. Helen Keller, blind and deaf from birth, said: "For three things I thank God every day of my life: thanks that He has vouchsafed me knowledge of His works; deep thanks that He has set in my darkness the lamp of faith; deep, deepest thanks that I have another life to look forward to — a life joyous with light and flowers and heavenly song."

We do great good with our joy, for this brings others to God. Joy is frequently the best example of charity for people who observe us. The lives of the first Christians were attractive because of the peace and joy with which they did the commonplace things of ordinary life.

A Christian home must be bright, cheerful, and happy, because supernatural life leads us to practicing those virtues (generosity, cordiality, a spirit of service) with which joy is so intimately connected. Our serene joy ought to accompany us also in our work place and in all our social relations. Many people have found the road to God in the cordial, smiling conduct of a good Christian. St. Thomas Aquinas wrote that "everyone who wants to make progress in the spiritual life needs to have joy" (*Commentary on the Letter to the Philippians*, 4:1).

When we say or sing, "Jesus Christ is risen today," we don't mean only "Jesus Christ was risen once upon a time." We mean that the risen Christ is all around us, in the eyes and faces of those sitting beside us, in the bread and wine of the altar, in the newly baptized, and in the people we meet all the time. He walks the earth today — teaching, healing, touching, suffering, dying, and rising. If we go seeking the risen Jesus with faith and hope and love we will find him. Seek him, find him, love him in every person — by serving their needs: then truly not only is Christ risen but we, too, are already living a risen life by his power and grace.

Tuesday of the Octave of Easter

Ac 2:36-41; Jn 20:11-18

The Lord of Outcasts

By the time of today's Gospel, the two disciples most beloved by our Lord — Sts. Peter and John — had returned home. St. Mary Magdalene was the first to come back to the tomb, which she found empty. The Magdalene was omitted from the Easter Sunday liturgy, because that day gave unalloyed attention to the risen Jesus. The Easter actions of this loving loyal woman deserve our attention, however, and we happily give it today.

Mary thought the body has been stolen. That the tortured body of Christ couldn't even have a decent burial was for her the final indignity. She looked into the tomb as though she might have gathered some further information from this new glance. All was nothingness for her. She couldn't tear herself away from that tomb; she stayed outside it and cried.

The risen Lord appeared and called her by the name she had often heard. She responded to his accustomed gentle tone. Mary had sought her dead Lord; the risen Jesus sought Mary. Her tears had at first been wrung from a heart broken and tormented; now they flowed from a heart exulting. She flung her arms around him, laughing and crying in ecstasy, never to let him go. Titian's painting *Noli Me Tangere* ("Don't Touch Me") depicts the moment when Jesus was tenderly and lovingly asking this ardent, extravagant woman to release her passionate embrace. Titian's painting shows Mary on the ground at Jesus' feet, representing timidity and confusion over the mystery before her. She was capable of not clinging: in paintings of Jesus being taken down from the cross, she is sometimes shown tenderly holding only his feet.

It was wise that she release him — and, equally important, release herself: the past becomes a prison if we don't learn to let it go. Mary must let go of the human body of Jesus as she knelt before him in the garden if she's to become part of the mystical body of the risen Christ. Because she was the first to tell the Apostles that Jesus was risen, Mary Magdalene early on came to be known as the "apostle to the Apostles."

Who was Mary Magdalene? Over the centuries, this wildly popular saint has been the subject of many stereotypes: as a prostitute, a courtesan and *femme fatale*, a penitent, a muse, a teacher and preacher, a well-groomed fashion plate, and a wasted hag in rags. She has been dealt with in countless books, plays, music (including opera), and movies. Symbols by which she can be identified have developed in art: a lotion jar (sometimes a perfume bottle, a glass carafe, or a liturgical vessel) containing the oils she used to anoint Jesus; long, flowing red hair (red signifying dishonor) either smartly coifed or hanging in frazzled tresses; elaborate gowns or rags; pearl-like teardrops flowing from an eye; and a crucifix, a skull, and a book.

She has served as a classic image of the redemptive and transformative nature of Christian faith, turning the abstract concepts of sin and forgiveness into realistic human experience. As a transgressor saved by the healing love and forgiveness of Jesus, she's a source of spiritual encouragement for other sinners.

There are three lessons to be learned from today's readings.

The first lesson is that Jesus is Lord. Peter, pictured in today's first reading preaching to Jews on the first Pentecost about the meaning of the Resurrection, asserted that God made the crucified Jesus "Lord." (Peter had first called Jesus that at the miraculous catch of fish, which so impressed this fisherman.)

Mary Magdalene, in seeing Jesus after his Resurrection, also called him Lord.

We take that word for granted without taking note of the powerful significance it had then. It was an exalted title that was translated as *Kyrios* in Greek, where the word meant "Master" or "Lord" as used for nobility. It was also a pagan title for their gods. And it was the word used by the Greek Old Testament for "Yahweh." The use of this title for Jesus, giving him divine honors, was virtually instantaneous because of the experience with the risen and transformed Jesus.

Our second lesson in today's readings is shown in Jesus' behavior with Mary Magdalene: the revolution that he brought about in the elevation of women. Many other teachings and actions of Jesus add to that revolution: for example, his admitting women to companionship when that was against the custom, his dialogue with the Samaritan woman, his love and respect for his mother, his cure of the woman with menstrual problems, his forgiveness of the woman taken in adultery. And he associated with women regularly: to Martha he confessed his divinity, to the Samaritan woman he spoke of his mission, and now to Mary Magdalene he confided his Resurrection victory.

The third lesson for today is the importance of life in the Church. It's moving, as well as astounding, that St. Luke says in the Acts of the Apostles in today's first reading that some 3,000 people were added to the early Church at the strong and compelling conclusion of Peter's Pentecost sermon. So awakened were the sluggish hearts of Peter's hearers to a sense of guilt that they asked what *we* should ask: "What are we to do?" (v. 37). Peter's answer was the same as that of John the Baptist and Jesus: reform, repent, and be baptized into the company of Jesus' disciples (v. 38). These are all *positive* concepts: a *metanoia*, whose many connotations amount to a change of heart, a conversion. From this comes a life filled with hope, joy, and love, and a sense of responsibility to care.

Our Church, at times as vacillating as Peter, but always as

faithful as Mary Magdalene and Mary the mother of Jesus and the Beloved Disciple John, continues to proclaim God's saving truth generation after generation. Our Church, still learning, praying, and overall happy, is the voice of God in Jesus. The Church that defined the New Testament is the same community of forgiven sinners in which we keep faith with God and with Jesus in the Holy Spirit to the present day.

Jesus is truly risen, alleluia, and lives in his Church today — in each of us individually and in all of us communally. When Queen Victoria reigned in England, she would sometimes visit some of the humble cottages of her subjects. One time she entered the home of an elderly widow and stayed to enjoy a brief period of conversation. Later on, a couple of the widow's worldly neighbors taunted her by asking, "Granny, who's the most honored guest you've ever entertained in your home?" They expected her to say Jesus, for despite their ridicule of her, they recognized her spirituality. But she surprised them by answering, "The most honored guest I've ever entertained is Her Majesty the Queen." "Ah," they said, "now we caught you! How about this Jesus you're always talking about? Isn't he your most honored guest?" Her answer was definite: "No, indeed! He's not a guest. *He lives here!*" That silenced her hecklers.

Vatican Council II gives these basic directions for finding the risen Jesus: "By his power he [Jesus] is present in the sacraments so that when anybody baptizes it is really Christ himself who baptizes. He is present in his word since it is he himself who speaks when the holy Scriptures are read in the Church. Lastly, he is present when the Church prays and sings, for he has promised 'where two or three are gathered together in my name there am I in the midst of them' (Mt 18:20)." (*Constitution on the Sacred Liturgy*, 7)

Life out of Death

A man met another at a convention. "Gee whiz, Max," he said, "I haven't seen you in years. Gosh, you've changed. You used to be fat, now you're skinny; you used to have hair, now you're bald; you never had a moustache, now you have one; you were short, but now you seem taller — gosh, how you've changed, Max." The other man responded testily: "But my name isn't Max!" "Oh!" replied our friend, "you changed your name too, eh, Max?"

Today's Gospel, too, is a story of recognition. It's one of the greatest of the post-Easter accounts of meetings with the risen Jesus. Cleopas and his companion were disciples of Jesus — not Apostles or intimate friends, but disciples: followers. This may help to explain why they didn't recognize him. Another reason for not recognizing him was that his body wasn't a *resuscitated* one, which would have been the same as his mortal body, but a *resurrected* one, which would be unique and different.

Had Jesus really died? Whether you're called dead or alive may depend on where you live. In most developed nations, once your brain stops functioning, you're considered "brain-dead," and "brain-dead" means truly dead, even if a pacemaker were to keep your heart still beating and a ventilator your lungs going.

But it's not simple. If brain death is death, how do physicians determine when someone's brain has stopped functioning? There's a battery of tests of brain stem reflexes, including checking whether the pupils of the eyes are sensitive to light and whether the patient's eyes move when his head is turned quickly. But in a fundamental way, there are no fully correct tests for brain death. Beyond medical and legal issues lie metaphysical ones such as: What exactly is death? Is it an event or a process? The law prefers to say it's an event, but some people argue that it's a process, on the grounds that different organs expire at different rates.

Anxieties have often abounded about premature pronouncement of death and being buried alive. Scratch marks on the inside of subsequently dug-up coffin lids gave evidence that burial alive did happen. That age-old fear increased in the nineteenth century to the point that wealthy Europeans built "waiting mortuaries," where their bodies could be monitored to ensure they were really dead. Devices were placed in many coffins to permit the not-dead-after-all to communicate from their earth-enclosed coffin with lights, flags, and noisemakers.

There was no doubt that Jesus, the victim of the cruel punishment of crucifixion, was dead. The two disciples in today's Gospel had stayed in Jerusalem long enough to hear some of the women's tales of an empty grave and the appearance of angels, but they didn't put much stock in that. Perhaps the women were a bit emotionally overwrought. The two disciples had left Jerusalem downcast because of their disappointment that Jesus, their hope, had been crucified.

The atmosphere in Jerusalem had been sad, so they had taken to the road, and on the way a stranger joined them. Jesus — the stranger was he — started up a conversation. The two disciples spoke of Jesus as belonging to the past. Soon Jesus had their full attention as he assured them that nothing had gone wrong; rather, the truth was that they had been unable to see the saving hand of God in Jesus' sufferings and death, as shown in all the Scriptures beginning with Moses (v. 27). How much more satisfied we would feel if only St. Luke had given us an account of precisely *which* Scriptures Jesus used, and his *exact comments* on them!

An educated guess tells us that what Jesus spoke of was the constant scriptural theme that's also the theme of the Easter season: that God reveals Himself unceasingly as the One whose characteristic work is to bring life out of death.

There was, for example, God's promise to Abraham that he and his wife Sarah, whose hope of bearing children had because of old age long since died, would receive life through a son in

whose descendants all peoples were to find a blessing. There was
the vocation of Israel to be a "Suffering Servant": constantly de-
feated and yet always raised up again by the Lord God. A dead
people were revivified from slavery in Egypt and from Babylonian
exile. Ezekiel saw the dead bones of Hebrews on a battlefield
being revitalized. The Psalms spoke of one who was beaten down
being vindicated.

In particular, Jesus must have shown the two disciples that
the Jewish Scriptures had foretold three things of the Messiah:
he would suffer, he would rise again, and repentance would be
preached to the whole world in his name. The two gentlemen
now before him, said Jesus (v. 25), were too foolishly slow to
believe these lessons of Scripture.

They met the risen Lord, as do we all, in many ways. They
met him through hospitality, which developed into the early
Christian monks' motto, *venit hospes, venit Christus*: when a guest
comes, Christ comes. They met him by way of the word of God
in the Sacred Scriptures, which he explained to them. Preemi-
nently, they met him in the breaking of the bread that is the
Eucharist. (To recognize him in this way they must have been
present at the Last Supper.)

When Jesus left them, Cleopas and his companion, renewed
and invigorated, didn't even finish their meal in order to spread
the Good News to the Apostles in Jerusalem. They excitedly
hurried back to the city late at night: a very dangerous time to
be traveling. In the Upper Room, they found the eleven Apostles
and a few other disciples strongly emotional over the risen Jesus'
appearance to St. Peter. When in the excitement they finally got
their chance to speak, they told the others how Jesus was made
known to them in the breaking of the bread (v. 35).

Among the things the Jerusalem group told *them* was another example of death giving way to life — how Jesus had appeared to Peter! Peter had during Jesus' lifetime shown his participation in spiritual death on many occasions, right up to his
threefold denial at the end. Peter had now had the chance to know

the complete Jesus — not only Jesus of the suffering and death, but of the risen life and the mystical body.

That's what later made it possible in today's first reading for Peter to confidently face a beggar, who was well-known in Jerusalem to be lame from his birth over forty years before. In Jesus' name, he cured the man. That helped produce a large audience for Peter to lovingly proclaim Jesus, especially his Resurrection.

Jesus continues to make it possible for us to recognize him. We today often forget that, just as on the road to Emmaus, Jesus is alive and by our side at every moment. Jesus is, Jesus says, Jesus commands, Jesus prefers — now, at this very moment. The road to Emmaus runs through every town! In our daily associations, we have the opportunities to see him in others. At Mass, he opens the Book of the Scriptures for us in the Liturgy of the Word, and he breaks the Bread of Life for us in the Liturgy of the Eucharist.

God's characteristic work continues to be to bring life out of death. Sometimes, though, there are barriers to that: problems in one's family, or controversies in the Church, or suffering, or the death of a loved one. Faithful sensitivity to the Scriptures and fidelity to the Eucharistic breaking of the bread can bring us to recognize the presence of the Lord and his bringing life out of death.

Thursday of the Octave of Easter
Ac 3:11-26; Lk 24:35-48

Burn with Love, Joy, and Wonder

Little Johnny was visiting his grandparents on their farm. They gave him a slingshot to play with out in the woods. He practiced, but he could never hit his target. Discouraged, he headed back for dinner. As he was walking back, he saw grandma's pet duck. Out of impulse, he let his slingshot fly, hit the duck square in the head, and killed it. In a panic, he hid the dead duck in the woodpile — only to see his sister Sally watching.

She said nothing. The next day, though, when grandma said, "Sally, let's wash the dishes," Sally said, "Grandma, Johnny told me he would help." Then she whispered to him, "Remember the duck?" So Johnny did the dishes. Later that day, grandpa asked if the children wanted to go fishing. Grandma said, "I'm sorry, but I need Sally to help make supper." Sally just smiled and said, "Well, that's alright — Johnny told me he wanted to help with supper." She whispered to Johnny again, "Remember the duck?" So Sally went fishing while Johnny stayed to help.

After several days of Johnny doing both his chores and Sally's, he couldn't stand it any longer. He went to grandma and confessed that he had killed the duck. Grandma knelt down to him, gave him a hug, and said, "Sweetheart, I know. You see, I was standing at the window and I saw the whole thing. Because I love you, I forgave you. But I was just wondering how long you would let Sally make a slave of you."

One of the morals of the story is that whatever we've done — lying, hatred, anger, bitterness — and the devil keeps throwing it in our face, we need to know that God saw the whole thing. He wants us to know that He loves us and we can be forgiven.

Some of our non-Catholic neighbors tease us about being guilt-ridden. Sometimes we contribute to that perception. Why is it, for example, that so often we observe Lent, the self-disciplining preparatory season, for 40 days while, in popular practice at least, we celebrate Easter, the season of joy, for only one day when the Church officially celebrates it for 50 days? The early Christians considered Eastertide the most important time in the calendar. Officially, the Church still does.

Perhaps the reason for today's ho-hum attitude is the lack of images to shape and motivate contemplation of the Resurrection. Much of the artwork and symbols of churches have focused on Jesus' Passion and crucifixion. The few artists who have attempted depictions of the Resurrection haven't captured its dazzling beauty, glory, joy, and humor.

But when Jesus' Resurrection took place, there were all kinds of excitement. Consider, for example, the two disciples who experienced the risen Jesus on the road to Emmaus. When with the disciples in Jerusalem they finally got their turn to explain Jesus' appearance to them, Jesus came and showed his glorified body. All in the room reacted just as we would: they were in a panic. Their historical age was no more disposed to believe in miracles than ours. From the sublime heights to which they had relegated God in His majesty, they didn't think of Him dealing with things mundane except to keep the world in its regular course.

Even when the Jerusalem disciples began to come around, they were still incredulous — but for joy (v. 41). It was simply too good to be true! So Jesus had them touch him and see the marks of the nails in his hands and feet (v. 39), to show that he was the same person who had died and risen. He then ate in their presence — not to show that he was restored to the normal life of growth and decline, but to prove that he was no ghost, or phantom, or figment of anyone's imagination.

To be at table with Jesus wasn't unusual. The Gospels often tell about it: Jesus had worked his first miracle by changing water into wine at a wedding reception (Jn 2:1-11); he was the guest of honor at the party which Levi gave after his call to discipleship (Lk 5:27-32); he accepted a Pharisee's invitation to dine with him (Lk 7:36-50); he made a meal for 5,000 famished people out of five loaves and two fish (Lk 9:10-17); he enjoyed the table of his friends Martha and Mary (Lk 10:38-42); and his most unforgettable dinner was the Passover meal he shared with his Apostles the night before he died (Lk 22:7-20).

Now, Jesus was enjoining his disciples to preach the Gospel to all the nations, beginning from Jerusalem (v. 47). Jerusa-

lem was the capital city of the old theocracy, the site of the
Temple of God, the religious center of the Jewish people, the
place from which the prophets had foretold would issue the glad
tidings of the new dispensation. The entire Gospel of St. Luke
told of the whole of Jesus' ministry as a journey to that holy city.
Now at the end of Luke's Gospel, the word of God was to go from
Jerusalem to the ends of the earth, to the point where today about
two billion people (out of earth's total population of nearly seven
billion) profess faith in Jesus.

An example of the beginning of that process is Peter's sermon in today's first reading. Peter showed the faith community's
love and respect for Jesus by using great titles to describe him:
"the Holy One," "the Just One," "God's servant," "the author of
life," "the Messiah" — and the Son of the Jews' God of Abraham,
Isaac, and Jacob. Peter placed Jesus' death and Resurrection
within the larger framework of the Jewish tradition: as the first-
born from the dead, the innocent sufferer who is the sole source
of the salvation of all the world. Forestalling objections from the
Jews who were expecting a Messiah who would be a victorious
leader of their nation, Peter reminded them that Jesus' sufferings
had been foretold by the prophets.

Our Christian faith embraces the realization that Jesus has
won salvation for us by the sacrifice of the cross, as in Peter's
sermon. When we encounter the harsh reality of sin in our lives,
Jesus remains our advocate. And in our pilgrimage of faith the
action of the Holy Spirit calls for a never-ending conversion of
our innermost selves.

We can help our road to God by keeping always fresh the
joy and wonder of Jesus' Resurrection on the first Easter. And
we pray for prophets like Peter in our society: that their words
and actions may inspire people to lives of holiness. We're mindful, too, of all who are searching for meaning in their lives, that
they will discover the Lord's presence.

Ac 4:1-12; Jn 21:1-14

No Other Name by Which We Can Be Saved?

After Jesus' Resurrection the Apostles had gone back to the fishing in the Lake of Galilee which they had done when the Lord first called them. Why did the Lord choose so many fishermen — and not, for example, carpenters like himself — among his Apostles? We don't know, of course, but one thing that he must have especially appreciated was fishermen's never-failing patience and endless hope.

Night was considered the best time for fishing. Now it was twilight. Other boats had already left the shore when Simon Peter told the other six Apostles who were there that he was going fishing. The others decided to join him. Was this business as usual? Or did they feel that they might get in a little fishing while there was still time before whatever lay ahead? Or was it that life had to go on, and they had families to feed and support? Whatever the reason, the event is reminiscent of the commissioning of Peter as a "fisher of men" in St. Luke's Gospel (5:1-11).

During that night, on their own, in the absence of Jesus, the Apostles fished in vain. (The same thing happens to us every day; the real tragedy for the Christian happens when things are done as if the Lord had never risen from the dead.) At dawn, the risen Jesus came to the beach to strengthen them in their faith. The tired fishermen were dejectedly returning with nothing, and they at first didn't recognize him. At about a hundred yards from land, at daybreak, they could hear him when he began to call. When they accepted his suggestion to cast their net to the starboard side and they caught so many fish that they couldn't haul them in, they were astounded, to say the least. This was especially true of St. Peter, who really knew fishing firsthand.

Something about that man standing on the shore, though, along with the enormous catch of fish, caused St. John to recognize the risen Lord. That wasn't as easy as it may sound: Jesus' body was, after all, a *resurrected* one, not a *resuscitated* one. His appearance was different from when they'd known him before. St. Bernard of Clairvaux describes our risen body as having certain qualities similar to that of Jesus: it will, he says, possess what he calls *impassibility*, not experiencing suffering or disorder; *lightness*, having none of the downward pull of weight; and *beauty*, so it will be clear and shining, with no spot of dirtiness. God will also grant an *agility* so great that in an instant we will be able to go wherever we want. In Jesus' case, he mightn't even have cast a shadow.

When John pointed out Jesus' identity, Peter couldn't wait to tie his loose shirt so it wouldn't float when he jumped into the water. For a Jew of that time, to offer a greeting was, after all, a religious act, and for it a man must be properly clothed.

Jesus, who had dined with them the night before he died, now that he was risen shared an early morning breakfast-on-the-beach with them. The risen Lord wasn't an hallucination or a spirit, but a real person: an hallucination or a spirit wasn't likely to cook a meal and share in eating it. Despite the scene's solemn glory, the Apostles took the time to abide by their routine of counting their fish, the usual purpose of which was to divide the catch equitably. Many scholars have used the number of fish and the unbroken net to symbolize the Church: its universality can hold a great number of people of all kinds without breaking the net of her unity.

Jesus can be recognized in the sharing of a meal. Bread and fish were the food he had blessed in the feeding miracle in the grassy plain (Jn 6:9). After his Resurrection, he had opened the eyes of the two disciples at Emmaus by blessing, breaking, and distributing bread to them (Lk 24:30). When in his risen state he had stood in the midst of the Apostles in the Upper Room in Jerusalem, he had eaten some fish to dispel doubts (Lk 24:43).

Today's reading from the Acts of the Apostles presents a Peter who was, after his experience of Jesus' suffering, more mature. Then, after Jesus' Resurrection and the coming of the Holy Spirit on Pentecost, he had grown from greatness to greatness; his growth, like most of ours, wasn't a perceptible, continuous, eternal march upward, but a saw-toothed progress: sometimes down but, hopefully, overall up. This unpretentious fisherman — before his association with Christ a blustering, imprudent, spontaneous, but generous human being — was now able to stand up to the wealthiest and most powerful body in the land.

These were the dreaded Sanhedrin — elders of the people, scribes, Pharisees, Sadducees, and representatives of the priestly families: the legislative, executive, and judicial branches of government all rolled into one. This group had exercised their power over life and death in handing Jesus over and persuading Pilate to execute him. Peter hadn't forgotten that, and he knew that in his own case they could charge him with his curing the man at the temple gate, which preceded today's sermon.

To the Sanhedrin, the preaching of Peter and the other Apostles was doubly serious: they considered the Apostles heretics for one thing, and potential disturbers of the peace for another. Yet the "unlettered" Peter now stood before the Sanhedrin, as Jesus had done, more like their judge than their victim. Peter's message was essentially that the stone which the builders — the Sanhedrin and other leaders — had rejected had become the cornerstone of a whole new edifice of salvation.

As members of that edifice, let's fully recognize Jesus our cornerstone, and courageously as well as lovingly pay him our homage by joyous lives of courage.

Appearances of the Risen Jesus

There was a young customs official whose job was to search vehicles on the road entering the country for smuggled goods. One day a young woman rode up to his gate on a very nice motorcycle. Strapped behind her seat was a large box full of sand. The guard sensed in his gut that the woman was smuggling something, so he emptied the box of sand on a table and sifted through its contents. He found nothing but ordinary sand. Without any evidence, he had to return the sand and let the woman go.

For several weeks, the same woman continued to pass through the official's gate the same way. Each time, he would search through her box of sand, hoping to find something. He never found anything but ordinary sand.

One day, as he was searching through yet another box of sand, the guard became so frustrated that he called a more experienced co-worker over from the gate next to him. The second guard glanced at the sand, looked at the woman's papers, and then arrested her — for smuggling motorcycles!

Sometimes we have to be astute to see through appearances. St. Mark ended his Gospel with eight verses (16:1-8) which give us a small picture of the Resurrection: Mary Magdalene and the other women discover that Jesus' tombstone has been rolled back, a young man in white tells them that Jesus has indeed risen, and the women flee trembling, bewildered, and afraid.

Dissatisfied with such an abrupt ending, a later author added a synopsis of Easter appearances from the other Gospels that we read today. For example, Jesus' appearance to Mary Magdalene (v. 9) is more fully described in Sts. Matthew (28:9f.; Monday of the Octave of Easter), Luke (24:10f.; Holy Saturday, Cycle C), and John (20:14-18; Tuesday of the Octave of Easter). His appearance to the two disciples walking into the country (v.

12) is told at greater length in Luke's story of Cleopas and his companion (24:13-35; Wednesday of the Octave of Easter). His revelation to the eleven disciples at table (v. 14) is related more fully in the other Evangelists, too (Lk 24:36-43; Thursday of the Octave of Easter; Mt 28:16-20; and Jn 20:19-23, 26-29).

In the midst of the general rejoicing that accompanied the second day of the paschal festival then being celebrated, Jesus' disciples remained sorrowful. They didn't dare believe what they considered as idle tales of Mary Magdalene and the other holy women about Jesus having risen. Cleopas and his companion, on their way home to their native village disappointedly, met the risen Jesus. It was only in sharing the Eucharist that they recognized Jesus, who then vanished. The two disciples, carried away by joy, spread the Good News as quickly as they could. At Jerusalem, they found the eleven Apostles reunited with a few companions, all under strong emotion.

Whereas Peter and John had returned from the tomb, Mary Magdalene wouldn't go away. She had been the last to leave both the cross and the sepulchre; she was the first to come back to the tomb. She found it empty. Now she couldn't tear herself away from it, but stayed outside and cried. For her, there was no one else. She had no fear, because one fears only when one loves, and her love was gone.

Pious Christians have no doubt that, although Scripture doesn't record it, the newly risen Jesus appeared first of all to his mother. She had fed him at her breast, she had guided him in his childhood years, she had (so to say) introduced him to the world at the wedding reception of Cana, and beyond that she hardly appears in the Gospels until she stands at the foot of the cross. But to her, along with St. Joseph, Jesus had devoted the roughly thirty years of his "hidden" life in Nazareth. Would he not have reserved for her the first moments of his new life that was hidden in God?

In today's first reading, the people found Peter and John preaching, though they hadn't trained in the rabbinical tradition and had no jurisdiction from the authorities to teach. They defied the civil authorities under the principle that they were going to obey God rather than men; because the cripple whom they had just cured was standing there, the authorities couldn't take open action against Peter and John. The two Apostles showed the extent to which the early Church was emboldened. Boldness connotes the freedom and confidence which the Holy Spirit gives His spokespersons despite all dangers. It's the mark of free spirits, and it's the trademark of the preaching of the Apostles.

The leaders' private consultation among themselves effectively illustrates the finality of their unbelief, resistant even to the popular acclaim of Peter and John's miracle of healing the crippled beggar. The authorities' threats revealed their moral powerlessness and spiritual emptiness. Peter's words express a compulsion to bear witness to Christ — the Way, the Truth, and the Life.

We update today's collage by remembering Jesus' coming into the world and to us in the word and sacrament of every Eucharistic celebration. Here the Good News is proclaimed and experienced every day.

Monday, Second Week of Easter

Ac 4:23-31; Jn 3:1-8

Speak God's Word with Correctness and Boldness

Today we read that Nicodemus was sufficiently troubled about Jesus' claim to have come from God that he approached Jesus. Nicodemus appears three times in the Scriptures (and only in St. John's Gospel), each time at night. His coming to Jesus at night has suggestive overtones: John the Evangelist will soon (vv. 19-21) establish the symbolism of two groups: those who come into the light of Jesus' presence and those who won't.

Nicodemus's night-time visit may be a hint that people were afraid to associate with Jesus because of the leaders of the Jews. Or his coming at night may indicate his stature as a true seeker, studying the Mosaic Law at night. Whereas the Pharisees' greeting of Jesus as "rabbi," or teacher, was sarcastic, Nicodemus used the title in good faith to show his respect for Jesus as a teacher from God. Indeed, Nicodemus's salutation shows that he put Jesus as teacher on a par with himself. This contrasts with the crowd's later rejection of Jesus as being unlettered (7:15).

This was the only time on record that Nicodemus actually met Jesus. Jesus always adapted his teaching to the simple capacity of country folk, telling stories to reach their level of understanding. With this more sophisticated man of Jerusalem, he moved the discussion to a more scholarly dialogue between existence from below and existence from above.

The story shows the continuing need of an interpreter of the Bible. This means having not only Scripture scholars and theologians, but also the Church, the "assembly," which was responsible for accepting the canonicity of the Bible in the first place. The Church decided, for example, that the difficult-to-understand Book of Revelation was inspired, but that such nice-sounding books as the Gospel of Thomas and the Gospel of Mary Magdalene were not.

Nicodemus was perhaps one of those well-intentioned people who put such an overly literal interpretation to the language of the Bible that they misunderstand it. For example, when Jesus assured Nicodemus that no one can see the rule of God unless the person is begotten *from above*, the phrase *from above* in the Greek (*anothen*) of St. John's Gospel can also mean *from the beginning* or *again*.

Nicodemus interpreted Jesus' statement as meaning that we have to be born *again*, thus misunderstanding Jesus. Perhaps

Nicodemus was using an opening for discussion. In either case, he asked Jesus how a person could be born *again* once he is old. Jesus corrected his misunderstanding by emphasizing that it was being born *from above* that he meant, not being born *again*. Sacred Scripture must not only be *read*: it must be *interpreted* correctly to get to its real meaning.

To translate the Bible into modern languages requires constant attention. American English, for instance, has been rated the most difficult language to learn, even more than Chinese. Take these examples. "Since there's no time like the present, he decided it was time to present the present." "The insurance was invalid for the invalid." "Upon seeing a tear in the painting, I shed a tear." "When the stars are out, they're visible; when the lights are out, they're invisible."

Jesus here distinguishes between "flesh" and "spirit." These are two completely different ways of life: one at the merely human level and the other in communion with God.

To be born of the flesh means to get what we can secure, use, and control: to succumb to the pursuits of "the world" in its bad sense. "Flesh" describes the human being as subject to weakness, sinfulness, and alienation from God.

To live the higher life, one must be "born of the Spirit." In other words, God's Holy Spirit is the agent of rebirth. Jesus speaks of that higher life as being carried by the wind. His word for "wind" is the same as the word for "spirit" in both Hebrew (*ruach*) and Greek (*pneuma*). The activity of the Holy Spirit is as mysterious as that of the wind, which blows where it will, and whose sound we can hear, but we don't know where it comes from or where it goes.

Today's reading from the Acts of the Apostles shows that, after Jesus' Resurrection and Ascension and the coming of the Holy Spirit, there was no mistaking the Apostles' correct interpretation of the Good News. They preached it so constantly and boldly that Sts. Peter and John were soon arrested.

Even after their release from prison, further trouble was in store. The Christian community prayed to their "sovereign Lord" — an expression acknowledging God's dominion over the whole cosmos. Yet they prayed not for freedom from persecution, but for the courage to continue to proclaim the Good News with boldness — in their Hellenistic world, a citizen's right to free speech. What's more, they courageously and pointedly applied Psalm 2 to those who conspired in Jesus' death: Herod Antipas and Pontius Pilate. Their prayer was heard. St. Luke, the artistic author of Acts, associates the earthquake, signaling the answer to the prayer, with the bold proclaiming of the Word.

The water and the Holy Spirit of our baptism have caused our new birth as children of God and His heirs; in our gratitude, we should imitate the zeal of Peter and John.

Tuesday, Second Week of Easter
Ac 4:32-37; Jn 3:7-15

Be of One Heart and Mind

A man of the road (they used to be called "hoboes") was hungry; he stopped in a vacant lot in a small town and decided to have some soup. Even while gathering materials for a small fire, he noticed children eyeing him from a distance. Taking a pot from his pack, he poured some water into it from his canteen. Then he started looking around on the ground. Finally, he found what he was looking for: a medium-sized white stone. The children were getting inquisitive. With broad gestures, knowing he was being watched (now by some adults as well) he slowly placed the stone in the pot. Waiting a few minutes, he took out a wooden spoon and started to stir the water.

The observers could stand it no longer. They walked over

and wanted to know what in the world he was doing. "Why," he said, "making stone soup." Almost in unison they exclaimed, "Stone soup?"

"Why, sure. You've never had stone soup? Best soup in the world," he said. He added slyly, "Of course, a potato or two would really make it special."

One of the boys watching said he knew where there were a few potatoes he could get. When the boy returned, the man, after wiping off and cutting the potatoes into small pieces, dropped them into the mixture. And again with great gestures the man of the road stirred the pot.

The man repeated the procedure with now one, then another, vegetable. Each time, with great gestures he cleaned the contributed vegetable, cut it up, placed it into the pot, and stirred it.

Time passed, and the stone soup was ready. The people were given a taste, and all agreed it was indeed a good-tasting soup. They also came to think that miracles can happen when a community works together toward a common goal.

Many of our younger generation seek to forge friendships in a society they perceive as increasingly hostile to the notion of community. Individuals are becoming increasingly isolated by economics, by housing, by technology. Youth sometimes grow up in broken homes, find themselves struggling to survive in a rabidly competitive economy, and have often watched the country's political leaders virtually abandon the notion of civic community. They want someplace to feel at home.

In the Acts of the Apostles, St. Luke describes the ideal Christian community as living with one heart and one mind. The one mind means union in faith. The one heart means love. It isn't only a *speculative* love that's important to show faith: today's portion of Acts mentions some *practical works*. If we have faith, we will have a sense of responsibility for one another and a real desire to share. We will develop deep personal relationships. We will, in short, be closer to the heavenly community pictured in Acts.

Luke's picture was idealized: not as the first Christian community was, but as he wanted it to be. It's a picture of the ideal that the Church should strive to become: a community of believers who are selfless and totally concerned for each other. That ideal was sufficiently attained so that the pagans at the time of the early Church could observe, "See how these Christians love one another."

From elsewhere in Acts, however, we know that in the early Church this didn't always happen: there were people who held back, like Ananias and Sapphira; there were squabbles between Jewish and non-Jewish Christians; and there were problems about the distribution of food, which led to the appointment of the first deacons.

Our Christian communities today, too, are less than ideal. We've neglected the needy and called it self-preservation. We've killed our unborn and called it choice. We've neglected to discipline our children and called it building self-esteem. We've abused power and called it our political system. We've coveted our neighbor's possessions and called it ambition. We've ruthlessly trampled over others and called it upward mobility. We've spoken profanities and called it freedom of expression.

True and lasting community can come only, as Jesus told Nicodemus, if it be born from above — from the heavenly Father through Jesus. Jesus spoke to Nicodemus of God having ordered Moses to make a bronze serpent, mount it on a pole, and enable all who looked at it to be cured of the bites of poisonous snakes as the people trekked through the Egyptian desert. In view of the Jews' First Commandment prohibition against graven images, that was strange. The rabbis explained it by saying that it wasn't the serpent that gave life but God, who commanded Moses to act in this way. The serpent was only a sign and symbol to point to God.

Jesus told Nicodemus that, for the salvation of the world, he himself would be lifted up. He meant this in a twofold sense: lifted up on the cross and lifted up into glory by his Resurrection and Ascension. Jesus told Nicodemus, and us through him, that if we look at Jesus and believe, that can give us eternal life (v. 15).

Jesus' "eternal life" stresses not the duration of life, but its quality. It's the highest life possible: the life of God Himself in us. It surrounds and infuses every aspect of our life with peace: peace with people because all are God's children, peace with life because we live in a friendly universe, and peace with ourselves because of a new insight into and humble acceptance of our weaknesses.

John the Evangelist tantalizingly doesn't tell us whether Nicodemus was converted to Jesus or not. He was a man of good will but, as is often the case with the intelligent — who perceive complexities and weigh arguments — he seemed to find it difficult to assent fully. His hesitation may have come from habitual compromises, or from his fear of consequences to his career ambitions, or from just plain lack of decisiveness.

The Evangelist, in his Gospel comparisons between those who believe in Jesus as coming into the light and those who don't believe as remaining in darkness, might be said to speak of Nicodemus as only coming *near* the light. Our natural curiosity prompts us to ask, "Did he ever step into the light?"

The more important question is, "Have we?"

We must constantly try to make true community happen. While we love the organization of the Church, at the same time we can't get away from our personal responsibilities. We can't assume that the system is all there is, and try to buy our way into it. A poor example is people in the Nazi organization: the Gestapo police officer who wanted to be the best officer he could be in rounding up as many Jews as possible; the train conductor who wanted to be the best conductor he could be, crowding as many Jews as possible on the trains and making sure the trains went faster; and the camp director who made sure the furnaces ran 24 hours every day.

In everything we do, let's commit ourselves to the teachings of Christ and his Church which we're called to accept. If we've become jaded, let's renew our vision, rededicating ourselves to the constant attempt to make our Church and our world what God meant them to be.

Let all of that begin with ourselves and right now: in the way we respond to the prayers of the Mass; in the loving respect with which we exchange the Kiss of Peace; in our reverence at Holy Communion; in our fellowship with one another. Then let's bring our community of faith to our homes, to those individuals with whom we've had differences, and to people who are at times polarized because of painful disagreements about Church teachings. Let's continue that by bringing about God's peace and love to our parish through concrete acts of loving service to the needy, the suffering, the housebound. That's true community.

Our congregation is a special and unique assembly, the visible sacrament of the saving unity to which God calls all people, the instrument for the redemption of all. It's comprised of the light of the world and the salt of the earth; it needs to be treated with respect and, indeed, reverence. The parish community is difficult to be around if we're not of one heart and one mind.

Wednesday, Second Week of Easter
Ac 5:17-26; Jn 3:16-21

The Great Escape

Jesus summed up his lesson to Nicodemus, about which we've been reading for the past two days, by saying that it was God who started the entire process of redemption, and the mainspring was love: God so loved the world that He gave His only Son (v. 16). God's total essence is love. His love isn't only deep, but broad: He loves the whole world — including those whom human beings consider unlovable. He even loves those who deliberately turn their backs on Him. St. Augustine said, "God loves each one of us as if there was only one of us to love."

Yet we often take God's love for granted — as we take grass for granted. Grass is the soil-builder of the greatest consequence, the unsung purifier of the earth's atmosphere. We play games on it, we mow it religiously, and we use it as carpeting around our buildings. Grass is the landscape of distance and broad open skies. It was grass which gave natural wealth — wool — to countries like England, and from this wealth sprang arts and power. Alas, however, the nutritious flower-rich meadows which generations of farmers had created were nearly all ploughed up or ruined with nitrates — all to make money.

Even so, there's the happiness with which we take to grass on a fine day, the way it's revered by sportsmen, its major role in painting, its near-worship in gardens, its place in the economy. Its beautiful green face has appeared spring after spring without fail. But how much we have taken it for granted!

We often take God's love for granted, too. Yet, even though God sent His Son that the world might be saved through him (v. 17), Jesus' coming inevitably provoked judgment. Some people condemn *themselves* by turning from the light (vv. 18-20). Suppose you try to elevate friends by taking them to a concert, or by introducing them to an art exhibition, or by giving them a literary classic. During the concert, your friends fidget; at the art exhibition, they look around at everything but the masterpieces; when reading the book, they fall asleep. The music, the art, and the book aren't on trial, but those who react to them are. What you meant to elevate has become a judgment.

St. John the Evangelist, in today's part of the story of Jesus' discussion with Nicodemus, makes comparisons between those who believe in Jesus as coming into the light and those who don't believe as remaining in darkness. We who are of the faith are called to be the light of the world. But what kind of light are we personally?

In the movies, eighty percent of what they do is close-ups or medium shots of the human face. Light is to movies what perspective is to paintings. A face filmed from directly in front will seem to be flat, especially if the light falls on it evenly. This circumstance is usually favorable for an older actress, because it obscures imperfections. To be filmed indoors sympathetically, a face needs to be lit by more than one light. A cameraman will often place a small light called a catch light close to the camera's lens. The catch light will be reflected in the actress's eyes. A face with no light in the eyes will seem remote, abstracted, the face of someone it's difficult to feel a connection with.

Cameramen pay much attention to the angle at which they light a character. Light from below distorts a face: unnatural shadows appear. Horror films and monster movies often have bottom lighting. Light from the top makes a face appear gaunt. The eyes go dark. The actor will look as if he were dangerous.

Among the other specialty lights specific to the face are kick lights and hair lights. Kick lights are used from behind an actor to show the grain and shape of the face. They're commonly used in he-man movies, to illuminate sweat on an actor's cheeks. A cameraman who is filming an actor with dark hair against a dark background and who doesn't want to see only the actor's face can use a hair light to make his hair stand out.

In most restaurants, we can find just about any kind of dining light. There are cave-like dining rooms where you must feel for your food, as well as bright, glaring places. In a good restaurant lighting, everyone appears to be under a flattering, wrinkle-concealing filter. The lighting can make the space seem as warm as a cocoon. There are also some beautiful rooms having a clean sparkle and shimmering light. These facets of light apply to our home, too. Light determines a mood.

Most designers recommend several sources of indirect light — sconces, say, and pin lights directed toward a painting — as well as light from a chandelier. And candles always remain a favorite. Clever candlelight can seem almost like hearths, with the surroundings dissolving in shadow. The candle's magic allure has never failed. For more reasons than one, many people would rather light one candle than curse the darkness.

And, of course, light and darkness clash in the universal struggle hovering between the supernatural world and the ordinary events of life. We see this in the lives of Peter and John in jail in today's first reading. God's message told the Apostles, in their escape from jail, to preach all about new life in Christ. The essence of this new life is in the first two sentences of today's Gospel: that God so loved the world that He gave His only Son for it, and that the Son came into the world not to condemn it but to save it. After being freed, Peter and John returned to the very Temple courtyard, preaching that message to an enthusiastic crowd. They were almost ignoring their deliverance from prison, acting as though nothing had happened.

Are we, like Nicodemus, coming only *near* Jesus' light? Or are we, like Peter and John, so much in and of the light that we're truly witnessing to our faith in Jesus? If we are, as Jesus asked us to be, the light of the world, what kind of light are we: catch light, bottom light, top light, kick light, hair light, sconce, pin light, candlelight?

Showing our love for God doesn't necessarily consist in sentimental feelings, although we may at times be blessed with them. Love for God consists essentially in the full identification of our will with that of God. It's seen in specific ways in the fulfillment of our duties toward God and others, even when our feelings don't incline us in that direction. Sentiment isn't bad, but the importance that is sometimes given to it is.

An ancient Gregorian hymn (*Creator alme siderum*) asserts that to the skies our monuments of folly soar. Daily, money barons and business tycoons build monuments of folly to their ambitions. We, on the other hand, are to say to God (*Roman Missal*, Prayer of Pope Clement XI): I want whatever you want, I want because you want, I want as you want, I want as long as you want.

If we stay in the dark, refusing to let God's love penetrate our heart, then nothing gets easy. Let's escape into loving God without limit. That's the whole reason for our being.

Thursday, Second Week of Easter

Ac 5:27-33; Jn 3:31-36

Enthusiasm in Religion

About thirty years ago near the city of Sao José dos Campos, Brazil, the government turned a prison over to two good Christians to run. The institution was renamed Humaita, and the plan was to run it on Christian principles. With the exception of two full-time staff, all the work was done by inmates.

Chuck Colson, important to prison ministry since his own imprisonment and now an ordained minister, visited the prison. On his visit, he found the inmates smiling — particularly the murderer who held the keys, opened the gates, and let Colson in. Wherever Colson walked he saw men at peace. He saw clean living areas and people working industriously. The walls were decorated with biblical sayings. His guide escorted him to the notorious prison cell once used for torture. Colson was told that now that block held only a single inmate. When they reached the end of the long concrete corridor to that cell, the guide put the key in the lock, and slowly opened the massive door. Colson saw the prisoner in that punishment cell: just a crucifix, beautifully carved by the Humaita inmates — the prisoner Jesus, hanging on a cross.

The guide said softly, "He's doing time for the rest of us."

In today's Gospel, Jesus is the redeemer from above, who inspires talk of heavenly things. God the Father has given him everything: among them judgment (5:22, 27), life (5:26), the power to give life (17:2), his followers (6:37; 10:29; 17:6), what he says (12:49; 17:8), the divine name (17:11f.), and glory (17:22). The Son of God in turn gives the Spirit of God without measure. Rejecting Jesus' testimony is the same as rejecting God. Jesus concludes his discourse with Nicodemus (v. 36) by dividing those who believe, who receive eternal life, and those who don't believe, who have condemned themselves — *condemned themselves* — to endure the wrath of God.

In today's first reading, Peter and the other Apostles were facing a second trial before the Sanhedrin. It illustrates Jesus' prediction that his followers would be dragged before civil authorities and have to bear witness to him (Lk 21:12f.). Peter spoke. This was one of his five sermons in the Acts of the Apostles. In stating that it's better to obey God rather than men (v. 29) Peter was close to Socrates on the same point (Plato, *Apol.* 29d). And he showed the immensity of the people's shame in laying violent hands on Jesus (v. 30). More importantly, for the first time he applied to Jesus the word "savior" (v. 31), that precious idea referring to Jesus as our liberator and the forgiver of our sins. In fact, he referred to Jesus as the very *founder* of salvation.

To the infuriated Sanhedrin, the powerful leaders of the Jews before whom Peter spoke, this made Peter a heretic. To them, Peter and the other Apostles were a threat also because they were potential disturbers of the peace. If there were an uprising, Rome would come in to re-establish order and in the process eliminate the Sanhedrin's prestige. The proud Sanhedrin weren't about to let that happen.

The modern opponents of Christ's followers, on the other hand, have discovered that killing people makes memorable martyrs of them. So the tactic of our day is condescending ridicule — putting forth the deception that the Church looks unrealistic, decadent, and unworthy of the belief of a reasonable person. Every human foible in the Church is blown out of proportion. The trust in leaders that's necessary for the Church's survival is attacked.

For us, as for Peter, recognition of Jesus often comes slowly; sometimes it comes in and through contact with others. We have all, like Peter and the other Apostles, responded in love. That often involves self-sacrifice, and sometimes suffering. One beneficial result of reverses like suffering is to make sure we don't get too comfortable, and fall asleep and miss our life.

Jesus' life and Resurrection show that through suffering and death one can achieve triumph. A little girl, upon finding a butterfly cocoon, brought it home. She waited with eager anticipation until the day for the butterfly to come forth. When that day finally arrived, a tiny head appeared, munching its way through the gray, paper-thin wall. She viewed the little creature with childish awe, but wasn't prepared for how long it would take and how difficult a time the butterfly would have. With a small stick, ever so carefully, she decided to help the butterfly. Within moments, instead of the hours that it might otherwise have taken, the butterfly was free. Then it tried to fly, but when it stretched its wings, it fell and died. "What happened?" the little girl pleaded, teary-eyed, to her father. "I even helped." "The butterfly needed that struggle," her father answered. "Without that, it was never able to strengthen its wings enough to fly."

The response of Peter and the Apostles to the Sanhedrin showed what they had become through suffering: men of courage, no longer aiming at "playing it safe"; men of principle, putting obedience to God's word before everything else; and men with a clear idea of their duty, which was to witness for Christ.

As we reflect on the Apostles' enthusiasm — a beautiful word from the Greek *en*, in + *theos*, God — to preach about Jesus, let's compare our enthusiasm with theirs. As Emerson said, nothing great was ever achieved without enthusiasm. Do we have a middle-of-the-road approach that's really an excuse for laziness?

Can anyone tell we're Christian by our way of life?

Peter's response must always be ours: Better for us to obey God rather than people!

Friday, Second Week of Easter
Ac 5:34-42; Jn 6:1-15

If It's from God...

People in many parts of the world hunger for food. Without minimizing the shame of that, hunger is much larger than for food. In a world that is in many ways unfair, we hunger for justice. In a world that seems on the brink of war somewhere every day, we hunger for peace. In a world of self-centeredness, all of us hunger for understanding, love, and friendship.

The greatest of all hungers is our hunger for spiritual nourishment. It's dealt with in chapter six of St. John's Gospel, one of the most momentous sections of the Bible, which is our Gospel reading today, tomorrow, and throughout next week.

When a great crowd followed Jesus because of their attraction to his miracles, he fled to a mountain top. Throughout most of Western history, at least since the ancient Greeks, many people felt repelled by mountains. The classical age believed in proportion and balance, and mountains were irregular and wild. The Romans found them desolate, hostile places. The poet John Donne, reflecting the general attitude of his age, called them warts on the planet. Martin Luther believed them to be part of God's retribution for man's fall, an outcome of the flood at the time of Noah, before which the earth had been perfectly round.

Western attitudes began to change when sciences like optics and astronomy provided a new, enlarged view of the universe. The change is best summed up by saying that awe, compounded of mingled terror and exultation once reserved for God, in the seventeenth century passed over to the greatest objects on the face of the Earth — oceans, deserts, and mountains. Our modern attitude toward mountains has evolved during the last few centuries to encompass a notion of the sublime in nature.

In the United States, mid-nineteenth century painters gave a certain spin to a new equation of mountains with the sublime. Nature was said to express God's infinitude. A view of the world from a place like Mt. Everest gave perspective for that. By the eighteenth century, awe and terror had become part of a new esthetic experience, exemplified by mountain climbing. Kant defined the experience of mountain climbing as "the terrifying sublime."

But most people of Jesus' time were willing to follow him not to a mountain top, but into the desert. There they didn't give a thought to distance, heat, or cold, because their needs were great. They sensed that they were welcome. They listened attentively to words which gave meaning to their lives, so attentively that they neglected life's necessities. So momentous to spiritual nourishment is Jesus' multiplication of the food in today's Gospel that it's the only one of Jesus' miracles told by all four evangelists.

Sharing food with one another is significant. Jesus made sharing food on an equal footing with *everyone* one of the key points in his way of relating to the world. Just think of the groupings who would normally not have eaten together, but who sat down together here: men eating with women, those who were ritually pure with those who were unclean, Jews with Gentiles, peasants with those of a higher social order.

Of all the facets of Jesus that appear in his attempt to satisfy hunger, two are especially evident: his compassion and the abundance of God's generosity. Although he had taken the Apostles away from the crowd for a well-deserved rest, when over 5,000 people came to see him he not only tolerated their disturbing his plans but, in contrast to the aloof abhorrence of the Apostles, compassionately welcomed them. Imagine your hard-earned vacation being disturbed by a crowd of hangers-on or unknowns coming to your get-away retreat to freeload!

Then imagine trying to cater a meal, even for ten, with, let's say, a loaf of bread and a can of sardines. At table with invited guests, a mother turned to her six-year-old daughter and asked if she would like to say the blessing. The girl replied, "I wouldn't know what to say." The mother told her, "Just say what you hear Mommy say." The girl bowed her head and said, "Dear Lord, why on earth did I invite all these people to dinner?"

The miracle shows also the *abundance* of God's love for *individuals*: each person ate and had more than enough, and there was a lot left over. Who received the fragments? Hopefully, the least (though not less favored) and the poor.

God offers the same abundance of results today to all who use the Eucharist properly. In fact, the overtones of multiplying the loaves and fish all refer to the Eucharist. The same Jesus who could perform this miracle could change bread and wine into his body and blood.

The Eucharist, the most exalted of all the Sacraments, is essentially a meal, like the one that Jesus shared with the people in today's miracle. It intends to bring together not only us with God, but us with one another. St. Thomas Aquinas said that the ultimate change that God sought in the Eucharist isn't the transubstantiation of the bread and wine into Jesus' body and blood, but the transformation of ourselves into Jesus' presence. Our communion means that we *receive* the body of Christ in the Eucharist and *perceive* the body of Christ in our neighbor. We can't share fruitfully in the first if we're unmindful of the second.

When as a family we have a meal together or participate in friends' hospitality, we have the opportunity for closeness with one another that nothing else has. In the Eucharist, God is providing the same opportunity. If we want the Eucharist to contribute to our spiritual nourishment — as Jesus intended — we must approach it with reverence and awe.

While we're urged to reverence and awe for all things sacred, the sacred seems to have long gone hand in hand with commerce. At the World Trade Center site after 9/11/2001, street vendors had rows and rows of knickknacks: snow domes of the twin towers, photos of the New York skyline before the terrorist attack, baseball caps bearing NYPD and FDNY logos, T-shirts vowing never to forget, NYC sweatshirts, Mets caps. And every day, people hawk trinkets on the outskirts of St. Peter's basilica in Rome. They sell sodas near the Western Wall in Jerusalem. Souvenir shops line the streets leading to Buddhist temples across Japan. There's commercialism in Lourdes, the French town of miracles.

On Good Friday in the Philippines, every year men are nailed to crosses to re-enact the Crucifixion. While the men hang from the cross, vendors at their feet sell ice cream and soft drinks to the crowd. Some scholars have speculated that similar activity may have taken place on Calvary 2,000 years ago. Evidently, you can't legislate taste, sensitivity, reverence, or awe.

Today's first reading tells us that there were members of the Sanhedrin who wanted to kill the Apostles for propagating reverence for Jesus as the Son of God. One man stood in opposition. He was Gamaliel, the grandson of the famous liberal rabbi Hillel, and teacher of St. Paul. Jesus and such of his teachings as the Eucharist are of God — so, as this reading suggests, no one can try to destroy them without fighting God Himself. Human movements come and go, but a movement that is of God can't be stilled — even by religious authority!

The celebration of the Eucharist reminds us that there's a balance to be struck between our personal little world and the much larger mountain of the mind of God.

Hope

Some researchers in the year 2003 made an interesting discovery of what had ultimately become of men who had been considered some of the world's most ambitious and successful more than two generations before, in the year 1923. They found that (1) the man who had been president of the largest steel company, Charles Schwab, died a pauper; (2) the president of the largest gas company, Edward Hopson, went insane; (3) the president of the New York Stock Exchange, Richard Whitney, was released from prison to die at home; (4) the greatest wheat speculator, Arthur Cooger, died abroad, penniless; and (5) the Great Bear of Wall Street, Cosabee Livermore, committed suicide.

St. Matthew in telling the same story as St. John in today's Gospel says that, after the multiplication of the loaves and fish, which immediately preceded today's Gospel, the Apostles' ambitions were such that Jesus had to *make* them get into the boat and leave. Admittedly, it's difficult to conform to *God's* way of thinking in the face of the earthly ambitions all around us. Yet Jesus, who always sought his heavenly Father's will, did precisely that.

Whereas in his moment of triumph Jesus went up on the mountain by himself to pray, the Apostles headed by boat the three or so miles across the Lake of Galilee to Capernaum. Hard-pressed by having to row against strong head winds in their little boat, at about three o'clock in the morning they saw something coming toward them on the water. It seemed to have a human shape, so the only thing they could think of was a ghost. They were more afraid of ghosts than of the winds, to which they were accustomed: the Gospel tells us they were terrified.

Tradition has seen in the boat an image of the Church in the world, tossed about by waves of persecution, heresies, and infidelities. St. Augustine said that when love grows cold the waves get bigger. Already in Augustine's time the pagans were saying that the Church was going to perish. But the knowledge that Christ is in the boat has always filled the faithful with a sense of security and peace. The attacks on the Church, the bad examples, the scandals, lead us to pray for those who are doing the damage, to make reparation, and to remain firm in our being united to the Church.

In our personal life, too, there can be tempests, threatening skies, and darkness — and perhaps some situations in which we should correct our course. These storms — interior and exterior — can be converted into occasions for increasing our faith, our hope, our charity, and our fortitude.

The tremendous work of salvation of Jesus and his Church takes place all over the world, beginning with the events recalled in today's first reading, from the Acts of the Apostles. Sad to see, this salvation history of the Church was, then as now, fraught with internal discord.

The first converts came from two groups of Jews, the Hellenists and the Hebrews. The Hellenistic Jews spoke Greek, the language of culture of the time, and on Jewish feasts and other occasions returned to Jerusalem from all over the Mediterranean region. The Hebrews, native Palestinians, spoke Aramaic. They continued to frequent the Temple and saw themselves as Jews in every respect. The Greek-speaking Jews — somewhat distanced psychologically, emotionally, and theologically from Temple and Torah — were much more liberal in their attitudes toward traditional Jewish customs.

One of the tensions between them was that the Hellenistic group complained that their senior citizens were being neglected in the daily distribution of food from the common store (v. 1) by the majority group, the local Hebrews. Another problem was that some Church members were so overworked in the service of the community that they were finding it hard to engage in important spiritual duties.

The early Church's solution was arrived at by prayer and discernment. In solving an internal problem, the Church achieved unity, not necessarily uniformity. New situations demand new forms of ministry. Here it resulted in the Apostles imposing hands upon the heads of seven good men before the entire community at prayer.

That was the origin of the sacred order of deacon. Though these assistants aren't called "deacons" here, their office is "deaconing": that is, service. Deacons were, however, to meet more than the immediate material need: later (Ac 6:8 and 8:5) we see two of the deacons involved in evangelization. The solution showed a Church with flexibility and growth, optimism and hope.

A young mother was ready for a few minutes of relaxation after a long and demanding day. Her young son, however, had other plans. "Read me a story, mom," the little boy requested. "Give mommy a few minutes to relax and unwind. Then I'll be happy to read you a story," pleaded the mother. The boy was insistent that mommy read to him now. The mother, with a stroke of genius, tore off the back page of the magazine she was trying to read. It contained a full-page picture of the world. As she tore it into several pieces, she asked her son to put the picture together and then she would read him a story. Surely this would buy relaxing time for mommy.

A short time later, though (too short a time for the mother), the boy announced the completion of the project. To her amazement, she found the world picture correctly assembled. When she asked her son how he managed to do it so quickly, he explained that on the reverse side of the page was the picture of a man. "When I got the man together," he said, "the whole world came together."

The responsibility of each of us to put our world together begins by getting ourselves together. Then we can become better friends, parents, spouses, employers, employees, students, teachers. We have to engage in our responsibilities with hope.

But hope isn't the same as optimism. By virtue of being conceived in a democratic country where optimism is rooted in our country's heritage, perhaps we're by nature optimistic. In 1840, Alexis de Tocqueville wrote that this country was built on "the indefinite perfectibility of man."

Yet there's a tyranny of the positive attitude, which tells people that there's only one way to be. Smile, be positive. You feel bad, and the optimists tell you you're defective for not being cheerful about it. Yet there's a positive power to negative thinking. The only way to correct what's wrong is to talk about it. A restaurant needs complaints or it's never going to fix what's not going right. And curmudgeons help society avoid complacency.

While there's nothing wrong with optimism, the theological virtue of hope is much more. Hope is based on the conviction that God is at work in our lives and in the world. Hope is, ultimately, a gift from God given to sustain us during difficult times. Hope is the little child that walks between the adults of faith and love; when the adults grow tired, the little one instills new life and energy. Hope never allows our faith to grow weak or our love to falter.

All of us faithful — the lifeblood of the Church — are called to serve with hope and commitment. Often, though, as with the Apostles on the lake, fear overcomes our faith. Let's leave ourselves open — truly and completely open — to God's way of being and doing in our lives and in our world. Then let's make our lives conform to what He wants of us.

Ac 6:8-15; Jn 6:22-29

Is There Such a Thing as a Free Lunch?

There was a little old lady who would come out every morning on the steps of her front porch, raise her arms to the sky, and shout, "Praise the Lord!" One day an atheist moved into the house next door. Over time, he became irritated at the little old lady. So every morning he would step out onto his front porch and yell after her, "There is no Lord!"

Time passed, with the two of them carrying on this way almost every day. Then one morning in the middle of winter, the little old lady stepped onto her front porch and shouted, "Praise the Lord! Lord, I have no food and I'm starving. Please provide for me, Oh Lord!" The next morning, she stepped onto her porch, and sitting there were two huge bags of groceries. "Praise the Lord!" she cried out. "He has provided groceries for me!" The atheist jumped from behind a wall and shouted, "I bought those groceries. There is no Lord!" The little old lady threw her arms into the air and shouted, "Praise the Lord! He has provided me with groceries, and He made the devil pay for them!"

In today's portion of the Gospel readings for these days, from the sixth chapter of St. John, the Evangelist is setting the scene for Jesus' showing that God's bread gives eternal life, and that the providence of God provides for people in life and in death.

Today's Gospel event took place after Jesus' multiplication of the few loaves and fish for thousands of people. During the night, when Jesus and his Apostles had escaped the enthusiasm of the crowd by rowing across the lake, the crowd had spent the same disturbed stormy night in the open fields. Despite the fact that the crowd's enthusiasm wasn't as great as yesterday's, they nevertheless followed him to the other side of the lake.

Jesus, knowing that what they were really looking for was

a free McDonald's or Burger King with perpetual fast food, by-passed the crowd's question of when he had gotten there (v. 25). He quickly informed these freeloaders that there's no such thing as a "free lunch," and tried to raise their sights. Reminiscent of his comparison of his words to running water in a country where water was precious (4:14), he now advised them not to work for food that perishes (v. 27). At this point, he wasn't yet referring to the Eucharist, but to his words of revelation.

They had enough faith to ask what God required of them (v. 29). He answered that their first obligation was to accept wholeheartedly what God does and requires. Only then was he able to inform them that they should be working for food that remains until life eternal — the Eucharistic food which he would give. The price is faith in the One whom God has sent. We abide by this every day we come together to be fed on Jesus' words and his bread of life.

According to the Acts of the Apostles in a few verses before today's first reading, deacons were to be men of good reputation, full of the Spirit, and possessors of wisdom. Stephen was all of that; he was one of the initial seven men chosen to be deacons. He was a man of grace and strength (v. 8), an exemplary Spirit-bearer of sufficient inner freedom to step out from behind the security of the letter of the Mosaic Law and proclaim his vision of what the coming of the Messiah means for *all* people. The message of Jesus was now being interpreted, Holy Spirit-inspired, in the new medium of the Greek language.

Jerusalem Jewry was at this time divided: one group spoke the Aramaic of Palestine; the other, immigrants from the diaspora, spoke only Greek. Some highly-respected Greek-speaking Jews took Stephen on in debate (v. 9), but they were no match for Stephen's inspired interpretation of the message of Jesus (v. 10). Unable to best Stephen in argument, his accusers falsely charged him with blasphemy (v. 11). It was undoubtedly true that Stephen and his followers being true to the teachings of Jesus had pro-pounded the essence of their charge. The leaders incited the people against him (v. 12) and made further false charges (vv. 13f.), while the members of the Sanhedrin intently stared at him.

The persecution of Stephen was a climax of the Sanhedrin's persecution of Christians, the first having ended in only threats (4:17, 21), the second with scourgings of the Apostles (5:40) and a resolve to kill (5:33). Now their hatred for Christ's followers was full-blown. Through it all, Stephen's face seemed like that of an angel (v. 15); this was a prelude to his final vision before he was killed.

Stephen is a lesson to all of us to stand up for what's right and true — though our bearing witness is unlikely to be as hazardous as it was for Stephen.

Tuesday, Third Week of Easter
Ac 7:51-8:1; Jn 6:30-35

Accepting God on *His* Terms

A man in the Bible Belt owned a remarkable horse which he had trained to go only if the rider said, "Praise the Lord," and would stop only if he said, "Amen." The man decided to sell the horse, but when he explained the horse's peculiarities to his buyer, the buyer said, "That's ridiculous. I've been raising horses all my life. I'll make him go *my* way." So he jumped on the horse and kicked him until he started to run. The horse ran faster and faster.

Worried, the buyer reined back and yelled, "Whoa!" But the horse wouldn't stop. Suddenly the man realized they were galloping toward the edge of a cliff. Remembering the seller's instructions about saying, "Praise the Lord!" to have the horse go and "Amen" to have him stop, he yelled desperately, "Oh, all right, *Amen!*" The horse screeched to a halt just in time. Peering down over the edge of the cliff, the man wiped the perspiration from his brow. "Whew," he shouted, "Praise the Lord!"

As we think of God — and especially in His Word and the Eucharist — do we, like the buyer of the horse, try to make God go our way or do we truly understand that we're made to go His way? In today's Gospel, even though Jesus had supplied the crowd miraculously with a free and filling meal the day before, they still wanted God to come to them on *their* terms (v. 30). They cited (v. 31) the manna that Moses had given as food to his hungry people on their trek through the desert as a sign of God's approval; they conveniently made no mention of their ancestors' dissatisfaction with it. Jesus told them (v. 32) that it wasn't Moses who gave the manna: it was God. And the bread of God's word gives life to the world (v. 33). Then Jesus startled them with his claim (v. 35) that he himself is the bread of life.

When we read St. John's chapter six part by part, as we do this week, we notice different nuances that Jesus gives to the term "bread of life." In today's section, Jesus refers eating his flesh and drinking his blood to those who come to him and believe in his teaching. The operative verbs here are not eating and drinking, but coming and believing. This is why at every Mass the Liturgy of the Word always comes before the Liturgy of the Eucharist. We open our ears and our hearts to receive Jesus' Word-bread-of-life before we open our hands and our mouths to receive Jesus' Eucharist-bread-of-life.

Jesus was clearly stating that he is replacing the Torah. He, not the Torah, is the way of eternal life. Unless we fill ourselves with him, we're not just empty and hungry: we're spiritually dead. We are what we eat. If for our intellectual and spiritual life we pursue only junk food like fame, prestige, wealth, or power, we shall die of intellectual and spiritual malnutrition.

Failing to know the prophetic word of God began with the world of ancient Israel, as St. Stephen said right before his martyrdom when he called the Jewish leaders stiff-necked, always opposing the Holy Spirit; he asked them which of the prophets they didn't persecute (Ac 7:51-53) — including their rejection of God become man.

Stephen saw beyond his audience whose faces were distorted with rage; he saw even beyond time, to Jesus standing at God's right hand (vv. 55f.) — a position of authority. Stephen's audience was no more pleased at hearing his mentioning the significant term "Son of Man" — knowing its implication of the divine — than those who had heard Jesus use it. Considering it blasphemy, they shouted in fury, covered their ears to hear no more of it, rushed Stephen, dragged him out of the city, and stoned him to death (vv. 57f.).

None of this was an official act of Judaism, since in Roman times not even the powerful Jewish Sanhedrin had the power to put anyone to death: Stephen's death was a lynching. The custom for such a lynch mob at that time before guns was to lead the condemned to a height and throw him off (as they had tried to do with Jesus at Nazareth). If that didn't kill him, they would hurl rocks at him until he died.

It was ironic that the participants in this ugly activity laid down their cloaks at the feet of a young man named Saul (v. 58), the future St. Paul, who for his part concurred in the killing. The fact that Paul, though implicated in Stephen's murder, was subsequently converted, suggests that God heard Stephen's prayer.

Stephen died very much as Jesus had. Both Jesus and Stephen were accused of blasphemy. Both were tried by a mob. Both were taken outside the Holy City of Jerusalem to be killed. Both died violent deaths. As Jesus had prayed to his heavenly Father to forgive his murderers, Stephen cried the same plea (7:60). And both Jesus and Stephen at the last commended their spirits to God. We pray that in the unjust ridicule we receive for advocating what is true and right and just — as, for example, condemning abortion and euthanasia — we shall stand as tall as Stephen did.

The case for euthanasia is usually made in sentimental terms like the following.

"Toward the end of my mother's life she didn't know who I was; she didn't know who *she* was. She was frightened: she kept calling out for her husband. He was by her side, but she couldn't recognize him. She suffered many afflictions, including incontinence. My father, who knew that she would have hated to be in a nursing home, insisted that she remain at home. Then in his late seventies, he looked after her 24 hours a day, and the task nearly killed him.

"If it had been our dog that had ended up that way — half-blind, half-deaf, epileptic, incontinent, unable to stand up, and without the faintest chance of recovery, I wouldn't have had the slightest compunction about asking the vet to put it down; nor would anybody have questioned the morality of my action. Was my mother less entitled to a dignified end than our dog?"

Yet a poll of 1,000 physicians some time ago revealed that a majority considered it impossible to set safe limits for euthanasia, and physicians are also mostly opposed to physician-assisted suicide. Such help could also have an impact on hospital staff. For example, it would have an effect on the drive to find treatments for cancer. Good palliative care — painkillers for the suffering — is hard to find where physicians have euthanasia as a possibility at the back of their minds.

In Holland, where euthanasia has been legal since 1990, a slippery slope showed itself. In 2001 only just over half of doctors fulfilled their legal responsibility to report their actions concerning euthanasia. And there were many cases where physicians ended a patient's life without an explicit request.

It's a sign of civilization for a society to give relief to those who are ill, especially those in a critical state. Palliative care is the key. Too many dying people (and their physicians) don't know what can be done to ease their suffering.

The first and foundational human right is the right to life, and the first duty of the state is to protect that right by safeguarding the lives of its citizens. Legalizing euthanasia or assisted suicide not only breaches this duty, but also radically undermines the moral and legal basis of society.

We pray for help to imitate Stephen's goodness and to love our enemies as Stephen did. We pray that in witnessing to truth we're not passive, lethargic, and indifferent, but zealous and eager to proclaim justice. We pray that we may have courage like Stephen's to be God's witnesses in season and out of season. And we pray that Stephen's kind of forgiveness will open lines of communication with unreceptive hard hearts and closed ears. We can't go very far toward loving God if we're unable to accept Him on His terms.

Wednesday, Third Week of Easter
Ac 8:1-8; Jn 6:35-40

Communicating the Life of the Holy Spirit

Communication isn't always easy. A judge was interviewing a woman regarding her pending divorce, and asked, "What are the grounds for your divorce?"

She replied, "About four acres and a nice little home in the middle of the property with a stream running by."

"No," he said, "I mean what is the foundation of this case?"

"It is made of concrete, brick and mortar," she responded.

"I mean," he continued, "What are your relations like?"

"I have an aunt and uncle living here in town, and so do my husband's parents."

He said, "Do you have a real grudge?"

"No," she replied, "We have a two-car carport and have never really needed one."

"Please," he tried with a new tactic, "is there any infidelity in your marriage?"

"Yes, both my son and daughter have stereo sets. We don't necessarily like the music, but the answer to your question is yes."

"Ma'am, does your husband ever beat you up?"

"Yes," she responded, "about twice a week he gets up earlier than I do."

Finally, in frustration, the judge asked, "Lady, why do you want a divorce?"

"Oh, I don't want a divorce," she replied. "I've never wanted a divorce. My husband does. He said he can't communicate with me!!"

Whatever holiness we have is communicated to us from our heavenly Father through Jesus by the action of the Holy Spirit. From time to time, if we have the sensitivity to perceive it, we're aware of what's happening as we share the Spirit with others. The Spirit is present in our common kindnesses, loving concern for one another, and bursts of inspiration. The Spirit's coming will happen whenever we love God enough.

Take, for example, today's first reading. Stephen had been put to death for his faith, and Saul was still carrying out his campaign of destroying the Church in Jerusalem. Yet what seemed to some to be the end of the Church was in fact leading to its strengthening and expansion. Providence made use of the persecution to carry the seed of the faith to places which otherwise would have taken longer to know Jesus. Persecution ushered in the second stage in the fulfillment of the commission of the risen Lord to make disciples of all nations.

Although the Gospel was spreading, believers were scattered. The faithful ones were aware of what Jesus said in today's Gospel about the necessity of believing. He called himself the Bread of Life; although we usually interpret that as referring to the Eucharist, it's also a figure for God's revelation of the Word in Jesus.

Today's Gospel reminds us that our bread of life, our spiritual sustenance, religion, is essentially about faith in Jesus rather than conformity to a set of regulations, whether ritual or legal. How ought we live life? By trying to get to know Jesus.

Jesus can show us our poverty, our misery, and the gravity of our sins only if at the same time he can show us the depths of his merciful love. When we have to reprimand someone and say, "You've done thus and so: admit it," if we show only the law and nonconformity to the law, that someone can't accept his sin. He will be crushed, and either find excuses or go away despairing. We must simultaneously show that the person is loved and that there is hope: that they can do better.

In that context, today's first reading shows the deacon Philip setting off on a one-man mission to preach the Good News of Jesus to the Samaritans. The Samaritans were hated by the orthodox Jews of Jerusalem. Jerusalem was a sophisticated city with great rabbinical schools, had centuries of traditions, was the source of continuity for the religion of Moses, had a large number of religious leaders, contained a great number of educational movements, and was the center for the governing body of Judaism.

Samaria, on the other hand, was neglected, oppressed, half-ignorant, and closed toward mass movements. To the Jerusalem Jews, the Samaritans were the "throw-away" people — somewhat like today's runaway children, pregnant teens, drug addicts, street people, and those who sell their bodies. Unlike Jerusalem, however, which persecuted the Christians, the Samaritans — open toward affection and sincerity — were receptive to and enthusiastic about the Gospel.

The contrast between the complex and unbelieving Jerusalemites and the uncomplicated Samaritans reminds us that a simple, unsophisticated faith is what saves. Do these comparisons mean that we shouldn't pursue learning? Hardly! We have an obligation to become all we can be.

Because Philip loved enough to sacrifice himself for God, many who were crippled of mind and body in Samaria were cured and, more importantly, the Samaritans received the Holy Spirit. And they were given great joy (v. 8). As happens all the time, love had worked miracles among people who hungered for it.

Our world needs love and the life of the Spirit as much as did the Jewish disciples to whom Jesus spoke and the Samaritans whom Philip met. There are many painful lives affected by broken relationships, shattered dreams, physical and mental ills, and torturing guilt. We must let such people know that they needn't be alone in their pain. Yet the same difficulties — sickness, calumny, hostile surroundings — will have different effects according to the dispositions of individuals' souls. Let's not be fainthearted in receiving the Spirit and in communicating Him to others by the witness of our lives.

Let's learn the art of communicating, so as to be effective in cooperating with the work of the Holy Spirit in spreading the Good News.

Thursday, Third Week of Easter

Ac 8:26-40; Jn 6:44-51

Greatness of Soul

A man driving on a back road through Pennsylvania stopped and asked a boy on a bridge with a fishing rod, "Tell me, how far is it to Mill Hall?" "Well," said the boy, "the way you're going it's about 24,996 miles, but if you turn around it's about four."

Often, we have to make a U-turn to achieve the greatness of soul to which we've been called. Great-soulness is interpreted differently by different people. According to legend, Norse warriors were ashamed to die of natural causes. Such a death seemed an act of cowardice. And so in his final hours a man would run himself through with his sword, hoping to convince the gods of Valhalla that he had been a sufficiently great person to have been killed in battle. An old and dying king would have his body packed onto a ship that was then set afire and put out to sea — thus going out in a blaze of glory. Men who set out on dangerous ventures were convinced that to die in that way was being a great person. Greatness in people means for us overcoming our narrowness and defects. Of course, just as water shares the good and bad qualities of the land through which it runs, people share the qualities of their lineage, locality, condition, occupation, and times in which they live. It's a triumph to overcome such limitations and acquire greatness of soul, or magnanimity.

Jesus is the prime example of greatness of soul, and his words in today's excerpt from St. John's Gospel — as his example throughout that Gospel — are preeminent. When Jesus speaks of himself as the "bread of life" in the beginning of the sixth chapter of St. John's Gospel, he means it in the sense of the food that sustains faith: his *teaching*. Only at the end of today's section, and in the conclusion of this important chapter, does he refer to his bread of life as being the Eucharist.

Jesus was speaking in the Capernaum synagogue. There's a theory that, on the Sabbaths near Passover, the readings in the synagogues of Jesus' day were taken from the early chapters of the Book of Genesis. There are, indeed, some parallels between those readings and Jesus' words. *Genesis* says, for example, that we shall not eat of the fruit of the tree in the middle of the Garden of Eden, lest we die (3:3); *Jesus* tells us that he's giving the bread from heaven for people to eat and never die (v. 50). *Genesis* talks of God driving us out of the garden lest we try to live forever (3:22); *Jesus* says that anyone who eats of the Eucharist will live forever (v. 51).

Today's excerpt from the Acts of the Apostles provides us with another example of greatness in people. One was a non-Jewish royal court official (whom Acts calls a "eunuch" but wasn't necessarily so in our physical sense of the word). St. Luke, the author of Acts, tells us that the deacon Philip, to whom the official spoke about Christ, was also moved to greatness by the Holy Spirit. This is the first account of a person of other than Jewish descent receiving the Gospel. In fact, the African origin of this convert, conjuring visions of dark-skinned people beyond civilization's outer boundaries, gave expressive evidence that the Gospel was truly on its way to "the end of the earth" (Ac 1:8).

Luke doesn't tell us explicitly, but the Ethiopian was probably a "God-fearer" — that is, one who accepted Jewish monotheism and ethics and attended the synagogue, but didn't consider himself bound by other regulations. The idea of his already being ready to convert to Christianity is given a strong backing by the facts that an angel going to Philip introduced the scene (v. 26), Philip was instructed by the Holy Spirit (v. 29), and Philip departed quite strangely when the scene was over (v. 39).

The Ethiopian was pondering the meaning of a text about the Suffering Servant of the Lord from Isaiah (53:7f.), which Christianity has always understood to mean Jesus. The Humiliated One has become the Exalted One and obtained an innumerable following ("posterity"). Philip explained the Scriptures so well that the official asked for baptism; Philip immediately administered the sacrament. The story leaves Philip in Caesarea Maritima (v. 40), his home, where a houseguest will later be St. Paul (21:8).

The two sides of Jesus' gift of the bread of life — his Word and the sacrament of the Eucharist — are a package deal. We need both Word and Sacrament. As with Philip and the court official, God is always drawing each of us closer to the greatsoulness that Jesus wants of us.

For that, we have to have vision, a commodity that's not too abundant. At the end of the nineteenth century, city planners in New York predicted that traffic would soon come to a standstill: there would be far too many horses, and too many tons of horse manure, for anyone to be able to move. In 1895, Lord Kelvin, president of the Royal Society in England, said, "Heavier-

✓ than-air flying machines are impossible." In 1899, Charles H. Duell, Commissioner of the Federal Office of Patents, proposed that the office be closed, on the ground that "everything that can be invented has been invented."

In 1929, Irving Fisher, professor of economics at Yale, said, "Stocks have reached what looks like a permanently high plateau." In 1938, the wise men at IBM told Chester Carlson, who invented xerography, that people wouldn't want to use a bulky machine when they could use carbon paper. In 1946, Darryl F. Zanuck of the Twentieth Century Fox motion picture studio claimed that TV "won't be able to hold any market after the first six months." In 1958, Thomas J. Watson, the chairman of IBM, said, "I think there is a world market for about five computers."

In addition to vision, we need the great-soulness to take risks. A professor showed a video of a baseball shooting down the left-field line, and the Yankees' speedy second baseman, who had singled in the inning, racing toward third base. With two outs in the eighth inning, the Yankees down by 3-2, and the ball caroming off the outfield wall, the third-base coach faced a decision on which the season would turn: Should the runner try for home?

At that point the professor stopped the tape. He had played this videotape of Game 2 of the 1980 American League Championship Series, and now asked his graduate students to weigh all the information before making their own decision. The professor, along with some of the country's top economists, psychologists, and statisticians, was researching a theory that resonates with the fans who scream for their team to go for it. Managers, coaches, and players were considered often too cautious for their own good. The same was found to be true in basketball and football.

The professors say that coaches and managers often seem to focus too much on the worst-case scenario. Travelers who drive hundreds of miles because they're afraid of a plane crash make the same mistake.

Blind peoples' world is bounded by the limits of their touch, ignorant peoples' world by the limits of their knowledge. Great-souled peoples' world is limited only by the extent of their vision and their ability to take risks for a worthwhile cause.

Friday, Third Week of Easter

Ac 9:1-20; Jn 6:52-59

The Eucharist and the Communion of Saints

A man who had been convicted and imprisoned for cannibalism twenty years ago came up for parole on the ground that his insanity had been cured. Many of the public gave rise to a hue and cry about the inadvisability of parole because of the heinous nature of his crime.

The complaint of cannibalism was similar to the complaint of some people about Jesus' teaching on the Eucharist; they asked how a man could give his flesh to eat. Is our communion with Jesus in the Eucharist cannibalism?

Jesus' real presence in the Eucharist is contrary to our *senses*, to our *science*, and to our *experience*. Our *senses* indicate that what looks like bread *is* bread, and what looks like wine *is* wine. Our *science* looks into the texture, shape, and composition of material things, and tells us that the host continues to possess the properties of bread. Our *experience* shows us that there's no way that we can look at a Eucharistic host under a microscope and find a tiny Jesus.

Nevertheless, the God-given reality is that Jesus *is* truly present in the Eucharist. There are many ways of being present. People can stand before one another physically. Actors are present to us on a movie screen. Our departed loved ones are present to us in our hearts.

Our Lord's Eucharistic presence is *sacramental*. The Church defines a sacrament as something material that brings about a spiritual reality. Thus, the bread and wine are not *symbols*: they're *signs*. Every sacrament has an outward sign that gives grace: the pouring of water at Baptism, the exchange of vows at marriage, the words of absolution in the Sacrament of Reconciliation, and so on. In the Eucharist, by God's power the reality of the bread has truly become the reality of Jesus' glorified body and the reality of the wine the reality of Jesus' blood.

Bread has been for humankind from the beginning the staff of life. "Bread" can also refer to the simple necessities of life. "Bread upon the waters" means charitable deeds performed without expectation of return. "Bread and butter" is associated with earning a livelihood. "Bread and circuses" are food and entertainment offered by a government, especially a dictatorship, to soothe discontent among the populace. The "breadbasket" of a nation is typically a grain-producing area that provides much of the food needed by other areas. To "break bread" means to eat and usually to share food with others. To "take the bread out of one's mouth" is to take away one's livelihood.

As for blood, the people of the ancient Holy Land believed that it contains life. They were familiar with blood sacrifices. Through this they dreamed of identity with others and with God. Blood is important today, too. Our dictionaries have entries under blood bank, blood bath, blood brother, blood cell, blood count, blood-curdling, life blood, blood lust, blood feud, blood-guilt, bloodhound, blood-line, blood money, blood poisoning, blood-pressure, blood serum, bloodshed, blood-stream, blood test, blood-thirsty. Hematology, the scientific study of blood, is becoming more and more important in studying the human body. And donations of blood are constantly sought.

As Jesus proceeded in today's continuation of the sixth chapter of St. John's Gospel, he made his teaching constantly stronger: "If you do not eat the flesh of the Son of Man and drink his blood, you have no life in you." And further along, "My flesh is real food, and my blood real drink." We're being promised true communion with the real person of the risen Lord, as well as with one another.

Today's first reading speaks to that. It's the awesome encounter between Saul (soon to be called Paul) and Jesus. Saul, a fiery and well-educated Pharisee, on his way to persecute the Christians in Damascus, was knocked off his horse by Jesus. That conversion is a decisive event in the beginning of the Church. The Acts of the Apostles repeats this story (chapters 22, 26), showing how important it is.

Jesus asked why Saul was persecuting *him*. From the earliest times of the Church, Christians have professed as one of the principal truths in the Apostles' Creed, "I believe in the Communion of Saints." This means that all who profess Christ — the saints in heaven, the souls in purgatory, and we upon earth — are united, and must be mindful of one another. The love that the saints in heaven — canonized or not — have for the souls in purgatory and us on earth isn't a passive love. The saints long to help on the way to heaven all souls, whose precious value they now realize as never before. And the prayers of people on earth have power with God.

The Communion of Saints goes beyond time. Each act which we perform in charity has limitless repercussions. On the Last Day we will be given to understand the incalculable reverberations which our words and actions have had. The invisible unity of the Church has many visible expressions. A privileged moment of that unity takes place in our reception of "Communion."

The people of the early Church understood these things. The Eucharist made a difference in their lives: it made it possible for them to bear each day. Today there's always the risk of having churches turned into museums. There's a great difference between a parish church that prays and one that has become a museum. Church-museums have no life. The measure of a parish church's vitality is reflected in its being a place where God is present in a special way and there's constant prayer.

The community that celebrates the Eucharist will be full in the measure in which we prepare ourselves in silent prayer before the presence of the Lord. One can, of course, pray in the woods. But if it were only that way, God's having possibly responded would remain an open question. Eucharist means God is a presence who has responded.

That's why, in Eucharistic adoration, prayer reaches a totally new level: now it involves both parties, and becomes really serious. More, prayer in this way is also universal. When we pray in the presence of the Eucharist, we're never alone: the whole Church prays with us. We're then before a God who has really given Himself to us, a God who liberates us from our limits and leads us to the Resurrection.

Saturday, Third Week of Easter

Ac 9:31-42; Jn 6:60-69

Personal Growth in the Life of the Spirit

It's always a pleasure to watch the growth of something good. One of the reasons for the attractiveness of Spring and Summer is that we can see the growth of nature: seeds coming into plant, plants coming into flower, flowers coming into fruit. It's also a pleasure to watch the growth of children. This is especially true if we don't see them for some time and can experience more growth than we see within the space of a day or week.

Today's liturgy points to the most important kind of growth — the spiritual. Someone once compared personal formation to building a skyscraper. If the first few stories are out of line, maybe no one will notice. But when the building is 18 or 20 stories high, everyone will see that it dangerously tilts.

Today's Gospel — the end of our current readings from St.

John's account of Jesus' sermon on the bread of life — shows the effect of Jesus' discourse. Our Lord had just finished teaching the most difficult but central doctrine of his Church: adherence to his word and belief in the Eucharist.

Despite all the wonders the crowd had witnessed in Jesus, now they observed that his teachings were too difficult for anyone to be expected to accept them (v. 60). That's a negative response that's still with us. The difficult talk is that Jesus is God's Word who must be believed; here it's also that he demanded that if people are to have real life they're to eat his flesh and drink his blood.

There were many possible concerns that caused division in the crowd. Obviously, Jesus' flesh for the bread of life was one. Jesus' claim to "give life" was another, as was his revealing of the "bread from heaven." Some who had been to this point disciples now deserted Jesus. They may have been willing to accept him as a brilliant and spellbinding teacher. And they knew him to be the son of exemplary parents, Joseph and Mary. But they were unable to see him as God, they couldn't accept his claim to "give life," and they couldn't believe in his flesh to eat and his blood to drink. The more things change, the more they remain the same!

If Jesus hadn't meant the Eucharist to really be his flesh and blood, he would have called the ideas back; he could have easily told the people, "Wait — I was using a metaphor. Let me explain!" Instead, each time he repeated the notion of the Eucharist he made his teaching even stronger. He amplified it by speaking of the contrast between flesh and spirit: between the natural and the supernatural. What's merely natural can't alone attain to anything that's on God's level, the level of the spirit (v. 63). Only the person "born of the Spirit" will be capable of accepting the truth of Jesus' words. No one can come to the Father except that the Father draw him (v. 65) — that is, through grace, which is supernatural. And people must cooperate with grace by taking the plunge of faith — by believing in Jesus as the ultimate word of the heavenly Father.

As if to demonstrate the truth of Jesus' words, a group of his followers left him. Rather than compromise the central doctrine of the Eucharist Jesus, now well into his ministry, turned to the Twelve (the first explicit reference to that term), those who had been closest to him, and asked if they too would like to leave. At Caesarea Philippi, Peter had responded with his great confession of Jesus' divinity. Would he come through again? The volatile Peter could go either way. After some suspense, Peter's poignant decision was to echo what Jesus himself had said about his words being Spirit and life (v. 63). Peter asked where else they could go, because Jesus was the Messiah, the Son of God (vv. 68f.).

The incident is one of the signs of the great growth of Peter. Nevertheless, Peter hadn't yet arrived at full growth. His confession of faith in Jesus was a dire omen of the rebuke that Jesus would have to direct at Peter as "Satan" for resisting Jesus' prediction of his suffering and death. John the Evangelist interjects in his narration the name of Jesus' betrayer and the horrifying fact that Judas was one of the chosen Twelve.

Peter's faithfulness was rewarded. Today's reading from the Acts of the Apostles tells us that, due to the change in Saul's career of persecution, the Church was now at peace (v. 31), and Peter was bringing God's Word to the Gentiles. In the early Church, Peter and the other Apostles were able to do what Jesus did — heal the sick and raise the dead. God granted these signs in order to strengthen the faith of the new Church which was just being born.

All was therefore in readiness for the conclusive phase of Luke's history — the Church's mission to the Gentiles. This had to be inaugurated by Peter, the leading Apostle, not Paul. Today's passage records two miracles — which evoke similar feats of Jesus — to fix our attention on Peter as a prelude to his epoch-making conversion of Cornelius, the first recorded Gentile to come into the Church.

The area of Lydda (Greek form of "Lod"), a town some 25

miles northwest of Jerusalem, had already been evangelized. As Peter testified (v. 34), it wasn't he who cured the paralytic Aeneas there, but Jesus Christ. The other miracle related here was the cure of Tabitha in Joppa, an ancient port city about 12 miles farther northwest of Lydda. Calling Tabitha "Dorcas," the Greek translation of her Aramaic name, shows this to be a Jewish-Christian story transmitted by Hellenized Christians. The stage was set for monumental events to follow.

As a parent nurtures a newborn, so too the Spirit nourishes the Church. It's still one of the great tests of faith to believe in a God who became human so that He might communicate His love for the human race, a God who leaves no stone unturned in making possible a growth in our relationship with Him.

Monday, Fourth Week of Easter
Ac 11:1-18; Jn 10:1-10

Attitudes toward Pastors

Some birds are artists, leaf-cutting ants practice agriculture, crows use tools, chimpanzees form coalitions against rivals. A major talent unique to humans is language, which enables us to communicate in detail and with precision. Yet some people are often careless about words. Take, for example, the Episcopalian vicar in a remote corner of England who one Friday e-mailed his bishop: "My wife just passed away. Please dispatch a substitute for the weekend."

Two important words used carefully in today's readings are "shepherd" and "guardian." The term "shepherd" contains within it the meaning of "guardian," but it's more tender. It occurs frequently in the Jewish Scriptures. Today's Responsorial Psalm (Ps

23) describes all of the things that the Lord our shepherd does for us his sheep. Christianity's religious leaders are called *pastor*, which means shepherd.

In today's reading, which is the only parable in St. John's entire Gospel, Jesus adds to his previous images of himself his being both the good shepherd and the gate to life. As good shepherd, he calls his sheep by name (v. 3). Among the Hebrews, sheep were most often raised for wool and for milk, and not for meat; so, like our domesticated dogs and cats, they became pets to the shepherd. Palestinian shepherds didn't use dogs to herd their sheep by nipping at their heels; they led their sheep themselves. The sheep would respond to the voice of their own shepherd, but to no one else. The sheep of God are able to discern the one who speaks with God's voice (v. 5).

Jesus must have been surprised when his listeners seemed to miss his point. So he tried to use the comparison of himself as the gate, or door, for the sheep (v. 7). In our time, we think of doors mostly as territorial barriers against being robbed or otherwise violated. Doors stand between public and private, between mine and yours.

But Jesus had more in mind. In modern terms, his idea would be more like an astronaut walking in outer space, umbilically attached to his craft. Seeing that his air reserve is almost gone, he realizes that it's time for him to return to his ship. He reaches for the hatch lever and finds the door locked. He desperately claws the bolted door. When the door is thrown open from within and he's pulled through it to escape into life, he realizes the importance of a door as the gate of life.

Jesus adds the warning that all who climb into the sheepfold in some other way than himself is a thief and a marauder. He was including all those in the Church responsible for bad leadership or foolish followership and all who try to use the Church for their own ends.

Have our Church's shepherds, guardians, and pastors, despite scandals, benefitted our world? For many reasons, yes.

Christianity bequeathed to Western culture a God who revealed Himself definitively in the person of Jesus, and who continues to redeem the world by the work of the Holy Spirit.

To a world ruled by fate and the whims of capricious gods, Jesus came in order that we might have life, and have it more abundantly (v. 10). At the core of the Christian faith is the Christian shepherds' teaching that the crucified Jesus was resurrected by God and promised resurrection for others; this is an enormous answer to the problem of death. Once death lost its power over life, life itself took on a new meaning, joyous and full of hope. The Romans threw people out into the street at the first symptoms of disease when they suspected it was contagious; Christians stayed and nursed the sick. You could do that only if you thought, "So what if I die? I have life eternal." The Christians who did most for the present world were those who thought most of the next.

Jesus' shepherds challenged prevailing notions of the virtuous life. Suffering, when accepted in imitation of the crucified Christ, was noble rather than merely pathetic. Forgiveness — even of one's enemies — became the sign of the true Christian. Where Aristotle had touted prudence, justice, courage, and temperance as the virtues central to the good life, Jesus emphasized such virtues as love, humility, patience, and peacemaking. Christian compassion was conspicuous in a unique concern for widows, orphans, the aged, and the infirm.

Jesus and his shepherds emphasized the individual, a crucial contribution to civilization. The sense of self deepened. In the *Confessions* of St. Augustine (A.D. 354-430) we have the first great document in the history of what Stendhal called "the introspective conscience of the West." Augustine remains to this day the father of autobiography, the first great psychologist, and the author who anticipated — by a millennium and a half — the modern novel's explorations of individual self-consciousness.

The notion of the sacredness of persons in turn led to new relationships and conditions: democracy, for example. Democracy — "government of the people, by the people and for the people," in Abraham Lincoln's definition — is not only a form of government, but a spirit. It consists largely in assumptions: one person about another, one nation about another. In our civilization these assumptions are Christian. From the beginning, Christians opposed abortion, defending both mother and child from barbarous procedures. In a less direct way, the guidance of Christianity transformed the way that masculinity was defined. In place of the dominant image of the male as warrior, Jesus and his shepherds counseled men to be peacemakers.

Nonviolence was, however, easy to espouse as long as Christians had no power. When Caesar became a Christian (an event never imagined), which he did when Constantine converted in 312 and Christianity became the official religion of the Roman Empire, ironically many Christians found it more difficult to follow their true shepherds than when they were a persecuted sect. Christ's sheep had to give further attention to principles of war. Augustine said that only defensive wars could be justified. They should be brief, a last resort, never for spoils or gain, always proportional to their goals. We're still a long way from nonviolence but, before Jesus, conquerors butchered people just for the fun of it.

As barbarians dismantled the Roman Empire, new shepherds and guides, called monks, copied the classics, thus preserving much of the old civilization and laying the foundations of the new. The monks founded the first European universities in cities like Paris and Bologna. The influence of Christian shepherds on Western culture survived also in secular form in areas like the law. Today, our shepherds help feed the hungry, house the poor, keep families together, protect the imprisoned, lead the misguided, educate the unlettered, and otherwise engage in overseeing rights.

Is the United States a nation that follows the Good Shepherd? Not in any formal sense: our citizens transgress Christianity's precepts freely. But the basic teachings of Christianity are in its bloodstream. The central doctrine of our political system — the inviolability of the individual — is inherited from two millennia of Christian insistence upon the sacredness of persons.

In 1911, the year before he was elected president, the historian Woodrow Wilson said: "America was born a Christian nation." Some presidents have referred to the need for religion; George Washington did that many times. Harry S. Truman said in 1950: "The fundamental basis of our Bill of Rights comes from the teachings which we get from Exodus and St. Matthew, from Isaiah and St. Paul."

Even the Supreme Court, so unpredictable in the area of religion, has occasionally given tribute to the benefits of following the Good Shepherd as guide. For example, in 1892 it said that "the morality of the country is deeply engrafted upon Christianity." (*Church of the Holy Trinity v. United States*, 143 U.S. 457 at 471.) In 1952 Justice William O. Douglas, speaking for the Court, wrote: "We are a religious people whose institutions presuppose a Supreme Being." (*Zorach v. Clauson*, 343 U.S. 306 at 313.) In 1961 Justice Felix Frankfurter declared that our "religious institutions have traditionally regulated virtually all human activity." (*McGowan v. Maryland*, 366 U.S. 420 at 461.)

The fight to adapt the guidance of our shepherds to new situations has been with us from the beginning. In today's first reading, Peter had to justify accepting Gentiles into the Church without any dietary restrictions from Judaism. The early Judeo-Christians retained the cultural prejudices of their background. They didn't understand, for example, how someone outside Judaism could be part of Jesus' family.

May our shepherds always lead us by example as well as words. And let's be positive in our acceptance of them, and actively participate in their work.

Sheep of Christ's Flock

There was once a bird, heavier and larger than a turkey, that never adapted to change. In the course of time it became flightless. Flightless, it became silly-looking and defenseless, and then extinct. It was called the dodo bird. People who came to look silly because they were hopelessly behind the times also came to be called dodos. It's a fact of life that we have to adapt to change or become extinct.

Jesus' discourse today, from the last of his lengthy talks to the people of Jerusalem in St. John's Gospel, took place on Solomon's Porch of the Temple — a roofed-over walkway with columns of magnificent pillars forty feet high where people went to meditate and pray and where rabbis strolled while instructing their students. It was around the Feast of the Dedication, which was associated with light, but it was winter, a time associated with darkness and death. The Pharisees were again asking, some in good faith, their usual questions about Jesus being the Messiah. His answers centered around himself as the Light and the Good Shepherd.

It's curious that God has often chosen a shepherd when He wanted to impart inspirations that revolutionize human lives. Moses, when he was in exile, was a shepherd. Jacob, the founder of the Jewish race, was a shepherd. David, the ancestor of the Jews' royal dynasty, started as a shepherd. Amos, the first Jew to commit his prophecies to writing, was a shepherd.

In the New Testament, the shepherds at Bethlehem were the first to hear from the angels of the divine-human birth. Just as God Himself was content to be described by His ancient people as a shepherd, the Lord Himself chose for himself the title of Good Shepherd. He handed the title on to St. Peter when he committed to him the care of all his flock.

In the early Church, no symbol, including the cross, was more prominent than the Good Shepherd and his sheep. That image, in our day seemingly meaningful only to a few rustics, isn't an antiquated image, even in our time of zooming airplanes, buzzing industry, efficient computers, and beckoning television screens. There's no better image to illustrate the intimate nature of the relationship between Jesus and us.

Whereas the image of sheep as applied to Jesus, especially as a lamb, signifies gentleness, young innocence, meekness, and purity, applied to people the image of our being sheep isn't very flattering. It often signifies that we're weak and in need of help. Sheep are among the dumbest of animals: they go into gullies, become entangled in brambles, fall into ditches, and wander into predators' territory. A sheepherder once said: "Sheep are born looking for a way to die."

No domesticated animal is as defenseless. Your pet dog likely as not has enough intelligence to find his way home, has some acute senses like smell and hearing to find food, and can defend himself against other animals or make a judgment to run away from one bigger than himself. Your pet cat retains many of the qualities of the wild, often owns you instead of vice versa, and is a loner with enough cunning to take care of most situations. It's been said that with a dog, you feed him, you give him plenty of affection, you take him for walks, and he thinks, "Wow, this fellow must be a god." With a cat, however, you feed him, you love him, you care for him, and he thinks, "Wow, I must be a god!"

It's neither of those ways with sheep! For us to *admit* that we're sheep is to put our trust completely in the Good Shepherd. We need connectedness with Jesus the Good Shepherd more than we know. If a baby is fed and warmed and cleaned but never held, smiled at, and talked to — all of which call the baby into growth into life — it won't develop normally. It's like that with our spiritual life and the Good Shepherd. The relationship between the Good Shepherd and his sheep is so intimate that it's an extension of the relationship between the Heavenly Father and His Son.

Jesus assures us that no one shall snatch us out of his hand (v. 28). To make us confident of our safety, Jesus tells us that not only does he have hold of us, but his heavenly Father does, too. How consoling! Whereas Jesus speaks of *his* sheep, forming *his* flock, being in *his* hand, he's also quick to put forth the heavenly Father's auspices (v. 29). In fact, Jesus makes one of his "hard sayings" that the Father and he are one (v. 30). Not "at one," but "one." He and the Father are one in mind, will, action, heart.

Jesus promises that his sheep shall never perish: physical death won't be the end but the beginning. That's part of the essence of the ever-old and ever-new Easter message: that God offers us eternal life, the life of the risen Jesus, the life of God Himself.

That offer is to *all* people, beginning with inhabitants of places like Antioch, where today's first reading reminds us that Jesus was preached for the first time to non-Jews. There Jesus' followers were called Christians for the first time; up to that time, they had been called "followers of the way." In Antioch, a Greek-speaking town in the Roman province of Syria, Jews rubbed shoulders with pagans. Those Christians who had escaped persecution had fled there as well as to Cyprus and Phoenicia. Conscious of its authority, the Jerusalem community sent one of its leaders, Barnabas, to help explore some of the difficulties facing what was becoming a multiracial Church.

The growth of the early Church entailed change in people's way of thinking and doing. That contrasts with some modern parishes' motto against change: "We've always done it this way." Think for a moment of the common railroad track. The United States standard railroad gauge (distance between the rails) is 4 feet, 8.5 inches. Why was that odd number gauge used? Because that's the way they built them in England, and English expatriates supervised the building of many of the United States railroads.

Why did the English build them like that? Because the first rail lines were built by the same people who built the pre-railroad tramways, and that's the gauge they used. Why did they use that gauge? Because the people who built the tramways used the same tools that had been used for building wagons for their horses, which used that wheel spacing.

Why did the wagons have that wheel spacing? Well, if they tried to use any other spacing, the wagon wheels would break on some of the old long-distance roads in England, because that was the spacing of the wheel ruts. Who built those old rutted roads? Imperial Rome, for their legions. And the Roman war chariots formed the initial ruts in the roads, which everyone else had to match for fear of destroying their wagon wheels. And the Imperial Roman war chariots were made just wide enough to accommodate the back ends of two war horses.

Today, if you see a space shuttle sitting on its launch pad, there are two big booster rockets attached to the sides of the main fuel tank. These are solid rocket boosters, or SRBs. The SRBs were made at a factory at Utah. The engineers who designed the SRBs would have preferred to make them a bit fatter, but the SRBs had to be shipped by train from the factory to the launch site. The railroad line from the factory happens to run through a tunnel in the mountains. The SRBs had to fit through that tunnel. The tunnel is slightly wider than the railroad track, and the railroad track continues to be about as wide as two horses' behinds. So, a major space shuttle design feature of what is arguably the world's most advanced transportation system was determined over two thousand years ago by the width of a horse's behind!

To find the fullness of human existence, we ought every day to adapt the Good Shepherd's message to the ever-changing circumstances of our lives. We don't, after all, want to become spiritually as extinct as the dodo bird or as restricted as the width of a horse's behind.

The Light for Full Life and Joy

A pastor saw that his church was getting into serious financial troubles. Coincidentally, by chance, while checking the church storeroom, he discovered several cartons of new Bibles that had never been opened. So at his Sunday sermon, he asked for volunteers who would be willing to sell the Bibles door-to-door for $10 each to raise desperately needed money for the church.

Peter, Paul, and Louie raised their hands to volunteer. The pastor knew that Peter and Paul earned their living as salesmen and were likely capable of selling Bibles, but he had serious doubts about Louie. Louie stuttered badly. But, wanting to show recognition and appreciation for Louie's wish to serve, the pastor decided to let him try.

He sent the three of them away with the back seats of their cars stacked with Bibles and asked them to report the results of their door-to-door selling efforts the following Sunday, which they did.

The anxious pastor immediately asked Peter, "Well, Peter, how did you make out selling our Bibles?" Proudly handing the pastor an envelope, Peter replied, "Well, using my sales prowess, I was able to sell 20 Bibles, and here's the 200 dollars I collected for the church." "Fine job, Peter!" the pastor said, vigorously shaking his hand. "You're indeed a fine salesman and the church is indebted to you."

Turning to Paul, he asked "And Paul, how many Bibles did you sell?" Paul confidently replied, "I was happy to give the church the benefit of my salesmanship. I sold 28 Bibles, and here's the 280 dollars I collected." The pastor responded, "That's absolutely splendid, Paul, and the church is indebted to you."

Apprehensively, the pastor turned to Louie and said, "And Louie, did you manage to sell any Bibles?" Louie silently offered a large envelope to the pastor, who opened it and counted the contents. "What's this?" the pastor exclaimed. "Louie, there's 3200 dollars in here! Are you saying that you sold 320 Bibles for the church, door to door, in just one week?" Louie just nodded.

"That's impossible!" both Peter and Paul said in unison. "We're professional salesmen, yet you claim to have sold 10 times as many Bibles as we did?"

"Yes, this does seem unlikely," the pastor agreed, avoiding offense. "Louie, I think you'd better explain."

Louie shrugged. "I-I-I- re-re-really do-do-don't kn-kn-know f-f-f-for sh-sh-sh-sure," he stammered.

Impatiently, Peter interrupted. "For crying out loud, Louie, just tell us what you said to them when they answered the door!"

"A-a-a-all I-I-I s-s-said wa-wa-was," Louis replied, "W-w-w-w-would y-y-y-you l-l-l-l-l-like t-t-to b-b-b-buy th-th-th-this B-B-B-B-Bible f-f-for t-t-ten b-b-b-bucks — o-o-o-or — wo-wo-would yo-you j-j-j-just l-like m-m-me t-t-to st-st-stand h-h-here and r-r-r-r-r-read it t-to y-y-you?"

In the Gospel of a couple of days ago, Jesus told us why he came into the world: that we might have life and enjoy it to the full. Honoring the pedagogical principle that repetition is the mother of learning, Jesus today repeats that purpose of his coming. First he states it negatively — he did *not* come to condemn the world — and then positively: but to save it. That's the essence of the Good News, the basic core of our faith. These encouraging words save many Christians from lives of doom and gloom, of fear, of joylessness.

Now coming nearer to the end of his ministry, Jesus openly gives a ringing affirmation of the theme of himself as the special Son of God. To reject him is to reject the Father who sent him and to stand condemned — condemned, it must be said, by our own fault. The real judgment of us is how we respond to Jesus' vision of human life and how we use our talents in the light of that vision.

As light of the world, Jesus causes the various values and

contours of human life to be perceived clearly, and so challenges people. Jesus approaches quietly so as not to disturb, to be present incognito in the full hubbub of the earth's affairs. If we have faith in him, we come to know the Father; if we don't, we exclude ourselves from sharing in the fullness of life.

The situation when St. Luke wrote his Acts of the Apostles, from which today's first reading comes, had changed significantly since Jesus' time. A second wave of persecution — this one by Herod Agrippa — had hit the Church. He had had St. James killed and had gone after St. Peter. But God, through the intercession of the Church, had helped Peter to escape. Agrippa met with a bad end. The Church was increasing. The "Age of the Apostles" was over.

The community had become convinced that there should be a mission to the Gentiles. But was that what God wanted? The early Christians' participation in the liturgy and their fasting gave them the reassuring answer of the Lord in the affirmative. The first missionaries, Barnabas and Paul, were designated.

One of their destinations, Seleucia, was the seaport of Antioch. For centuries it was one of the world's most important cities. In the days when Antioch was a thriving way station on the Silk Road and a crossroad of civilization, when it played host to visitors like Julius Caesar and was the capital of Syria and a center of the Byzantine Empire, no one could have imagined the obscurity and irrelevance into which it would fall. Today even most Turks consider Antakya, its modern name, remote and undistinguished.

When it was Antioch, however, its glory shone throughout the known world. Alexander the Great passed through in 333 B.C. and is said to have chosen the site on which Antioch was built. Before long it had become a bustling city. Antioch's golden age began when it was annexed to the Roman Empire in 64 B.C. Its population rose to more than half a million and it boasted a large amphitheater, a public bath, an elaborate network of aqueducts and sewage pipes, its own granary and weapons factory, a famous school of Greek philosophy, and a two-mile colonnaded avenue that was the longest and grandest in the world.

Antioch also played a crucial role in the early history of Christianity. As we saw yesterday, it was here at Antioch that the disciples were called Christians for the first time (Ac 11:26). Christianity thrived in Antioch, with setbacks like the decision of its citizens in the year 115 to hold the local bishop, St. Ignatius, responsible for an earthquake and feed him to lions.

That decision (obviously) did little good: Antioch was later shaken by a series of even more devastating quakes. The quakes, combined with a series of lost battles over the centuries in which citizens were massacred by Persians, Crusaders, and other enemies, reduced the city to a miserable village inhabited by just a few hundred people in rude huts. Only vines and lizards remained to mourn for a splendor that had gone forever.

Residents of today's New York, Paris, London, Moscow, Berlin, Rome, and other great metropolises who assume that their glories will last forever might take a cautionary lesson from ancient Antioch. Even in our so-called "great" modern cities, similar disasters can occur. A war or depression or natural disaster like lack of water can strike, then people disperse, and soon a city and its culture are lost forever.

If we want to receive God's light for the fullness of life and joy, let's first realize that Jesus' words in the Scriptures are God's word to us, and we come to understand that word more fully in prayer. We look for confirmation of that word in other events of our life: for example, conversations with our fellow Christians about God's word. Then we can look into the direction our life has been taking and act on our discernment.

And remember the African proverb: If you think you're too small to make a difference, try sleeping in a closed room with a mosquito.

Ac 13:13-25; Jn 13:16-20

Good News to God's People

A story is told of an orphaned boy who was living with his grand-mother when their house caught fire. The grandmother, trying to get upstairs to rescue the boy, died in the flames. The boy's cries for help were finally answered: a man climbed an iron drain-pipe and came down with the boy hanging tightly to his neck.

Several weeks later, a public hearing was held to determine who would receive custody of the child. A farmer, a teacher, and the town's wealthiest citizen all gave reasons they felt they should be chosen to give the boy a home. As they talked, the boy's eyes remained focused on the floor.

Then a stranger walked to the front to plead for custody of the boy. He slowly took his hands from his pockets, revealing the scars on them. As the crowd gasped, the boy cried out in rec-ognition. This was the man who had saved his life and whose hands had been burned when he climbed the hot drainpipe. With a leap the boy threw his arms around the man's neck and held on for dear life. The other men silently walked away, leaving the boy and his rescuer alone. Those marred hands had settled the issue of adoption.

Part of the essence of the ever-old and ever-new Easter message is that Jesus died to save us. God offers us eternal life, the life of the risen Jesus, the life of God Himself. That's Good News — news because it's something which never happened before, and good because it concerns what all human beings hold most dear: eternal life.

The eternal life Jesus offers isn't simply ordinary human life without end, but the fullness of human existence. To find that fullness, we ought every day to adapt Jesus' message to the ever-changing circumstances of our lives. In today's Gospel, which took place at the Last Supper, Jesus is concerned with service, love, humility, and mercy. He has just completed the washing of the disciples' feet, an act of unity and humility for his followers.

In today's first reading St. Paul makes the point that the coming of Jesus was the consummation of history. For Paul, history wasn't always going in circles, as his contemporary pagans thought, nor cynical, like the modern version that says history is but the record from life's winners about the follies of the losers. For Paul and us, history is going somewhere, in accordance with the purposes of God, even though those purposes may at times be unfathomable to us.

The synagogue was always the first place in any town at which Paul stopped. At the synagogue in Antioch, Paul took advantage of the usual synagogue protocol to address the congregation after the readings. His audience wasn't only Jews, but also Gentiles who frequented the synagogue through their congeniality with Judaism, but who weren't circumcised and weren't totally committed to Judaism. For Paul, they were fertile soil for conversion to Christianity.

He recounted the stories by which we might recognize that our God is a God who has been revealed through history and that the death and Resurrection of Jesus gave a new meaning to that history. Although some people, in their blind folly, rejected and crucified Jesus, Jesus rose, as we will rise, by the invincible power of Almighty God and to His eternal glory.

The final point in the sermons of Paul, as for Peter, is that Christ's coming is Good News to all whose hearts are ready and open. The Good News was received first by Jews who lived according to the Mosaic Law, and then by all people of good will who try to live according to God's law.

But what's Good News for people of open heart, listening ear, and upturned eye is bad news for those who sense only empty words. They don't feel the heartbeat of the message that could pulsate life into them. Jesus still speaks, but they, sad and unconverted, don't hear his voice. Good News is ours, if we but accept it. Good News is our neighbors', if we will share it.

As today's reading from the Acts of the Apostles shows, it's sometimes difficult for the flock to be mindful. To get to Antioch in Pisidia, which is slightly south of center in modern Turkey and almost 4,000 feet above sea-level, Paul and Barnabas had to go by one of the roughest roads in Asia Minor. Not only was it mountainous, but it was infested by brigands. The town was very mixed in population and therefore highly flammable. One thing that would easily inflame the considerable number of Jews who lived there was any expression that anybody but themselves were eligible for God's promises.

Despite that narrowness, Paul's synagogue sermon — his first sermon, an inaugural address, a turning point in the Church's work of evangelization — stressed important doctrines about Jesus: that his coming was the culmination of history; people didn't recognize that fact; although Jesus was crucified and died, he rose from the dead; his Resurrection was the fulfillment of prophecy; for people who were trying to change, Jesus' message is good news; for those who wouldn't change, Jesus' message is bad news. The reaction of the people was enthusiastic.

For the next three weeks — the remainder of the Easter season — our Gospel readings will treat us to parts of Jesus' discourse at his Last Supper. Like the last speeches of such famous figures of the Old Testament as Jacob (see Gn 47-49), Joshua (see Jos 22-24), David (see 1 Ch 28-29), and Moses (see Dt), these remarks of Jesus express his parting feelings. It's our privilege to listen to what Jesus taught and to live it.

Today's portion took place right after Jesus had washed the disciples' feet, a job considered too lowly even for servants to do. Jesus, perhaps sensing the astonishment of the Apostles, reminded them (v. 16) that they, too, should be humble. Then (v. 19) he admonishes that through his betrayal, suffering, and death, they're to remember that he is God: the I AM. He's the one with the wounded hands who has saved us.

Ac 13:26-33; Jn 14:1-6

Living Life to the Fullest

An unschooled man watched from the curb as a large funeral cortege went by with a half-block-long hearse, ten flower cars, and twenty-five limousines filled with mourners. Finally, unable to contain his wonderment, he said to the man next to him, "Man, that's livin'!" Living life to the fullest doesn't mean fame and fortune when we die.

Nor does it mean living life longer. Some biologists believe it's only a question of time before they will be able to extend the life of humans. They think the normal human life span can eventually extend up to perhaps 200 years.

Actually, even if genetic engineering could elongate life, many undesirable features would accompany it. It would inevitably worsen many social crises already looming. It would increase population, further burdening the planet. And it's hard to imagine the government authorizing Medicaid to provide poor people with the genes for living an extra century or two. It's equally difficult to envision HMO's offering the genetic enhancement either, since if you live longer, you'll further burden its services and tax its profits. Further, it would have a potentially dire impact on work patterns, parenthood, the social security system, and species renewal.

True living comes not from prolonging life, but from making it possible to become all that we can be. That comes from being educated — not just schooled — in the right way. "What's the difference," someone once asked Aristotle, "between an educated and an uneducated man?" "The same difference," he replied, "as between being alive and being dead."

Today's liturgy tells us what the *fullest* living is about. The Gospel — appropriately for this Paschal season — is from a part of Jesus' profound farewell discourse at the Last Supper. Mind-

ful perhaps of the betrayal of Judas, Jesus counsels us not to let
our hearts be troubled (v. 1).

Jesus was about to be murdered, but his death would result in victory. In his Father's house there are many dwelling
places (v. 2), where he and his faithful followers will be together.
Jesus' departure is in order that he might prepare a place for each
of us, a place where we will be eternally at home. We all know
the comfort, peace, and well-being of being together "at home,"
especially at family feasts like Christmas, Thanksgiving, and
Easter. Further reassurance comes with his promise that he would
return from death (v. 3) and give new life.

He tells us that we know the way to the Father (v. 4). When
we travel, to insure places to stay we make advance reservations.
Today Jesus gives us a guarantee that he has made reservations
for us at our last resting place. Beyond what any travel agent
would do, he goes ahead to check out our place. He gives it a
special name: "My Father's House." And since Jesus' heavenly
Father is also "Our Father," we too can call it "Our Father's
House." The name brings to mind all the warm images of home:
a place where we're always welcome, a comfortable place where
we feel safe and secure, a place where we can just be ourselves.

And he does one more favor for us, his tired travelers: he
takes us there himself. Much more than a map, a directory, or a
highway sign, *he* is our way! In reply to Thomas' honest question, "How can we know the way?" (v. 5), Jesus declared that *he*
is the way. Jesus is for us, his people, as he had said so often, the
way to the Father, both by example and by identification with
the Father. In addition to that, he's also the truth and the life (v.
6). He's the *truth*, since in his Jewish usage the *true* signifies the
divine order, as distinguished from the deceptive disorder of
humankind. He's the *life* — that is, not mere existence, but sharing in the very life of God and communicating that life.

Jesus Christ alone reveals the Father, in the *way* he lives, in
the *truth* of his word, and in the quality of new *life* that he brings.
Yet he's close to us. When God became man he became not a king,

a chieftain, a warrior, statesman or great leader of nations, as some
had thought the Messiah would be, but a workingman. The Gospels show us Jesus the teacher, the healer, the wonderworker, but
these activities of his public life were the work of three short years.
For all the rest of his life on earth, God was a village carpenter.
He fashioned benches and tables and beds and roof beams and
plows, by hammer and saw, by ax and hatchet.

He worked long hours to help his father and then became
the support of his widowed mother, by the rough work of a hill
country craftsman. He worked in a shop every day, week in and
week out, for some twenty years. He did the routine (and perhaps often boring) work most of us have to do in our lifetimes.
There's little we can say about the jobs we do that couldn't be
said of the work God himself did when he became a man. And
he didn't think it beneath him. Rather, he restored to man's work
its original dignity, its essential function as a share in God's creative act.

His work wasn't merely a symbolic action like that of the
politician who turns the first spadeful of earth at a ground-break-
ing ceremony. He worked to show us that simple household tasks
and the repetitious work of the wage earner can be noble and
redemptive works worthy of God himself. He did it to make it
clear that the plainest and dullest of jobs is — or can be, if viewed
properly with respect to God and to eternity — a sharing in the
divine work of creation and redemption.

Living life to the fullest isn't only a compound of articles of
faith and commandments, but the expression of our total relationship with the whole of creation — and the core of this relationship is Christ. His work of salvation takes place all over the
world, beginning with the events recalled in today's reading from
the Acts of the Apostles, when St. Paul got up in the synagogue
at Antioch and gave a synopsis of what Jesus was all about. In a
sermon that was typical of the kind of missionary sermons given
to Jewish communities around the then-known world, Paul made
repentance and reconciliation understandable to the Jews by

speaking in terms of their own history. He told the story of the Jews up to David and then skipped to Jesus and the events of his Passion. Paul also added a small polemic against the spiritual blindness of Jerusalem officialdom. In including among his addressees all who reverence the God of the Jews, Paul was opening the Good News to Gentiles as well as Jews.

God's promise is to enable all people to live life to the fullest.

Saturday, Fourth Week of Easter

Ac 13:44-52; Jn 14:7-14

See Jesus, See God

Someone once said that we see God in the country, and Jesus in the city. His idea was that we see God in the wonders of nature: awesome stars, majestic mountains, a beautiful lake. We see Jesus, though, in the way people love and help the needy in Jesus' name — and, indeed, in the needy themselves, with whom Jesus identifies.

We want to have our daily living be a reflection of God in Jesus. It's not enough to have a general idea of the spirit of Jesus' life; we have to contemplate the details of that life. To know Jesus' blessed humanity better and to love him more, we read the Bible. But we can't read it as though it's just another book. In the sacred books our heavenly Father comes lovingly to meet us and talk with us. There we find a lasting font of spiritual life. We can't truthfully say that those who knew Jesus in real life were more fortunate than we. Some of those who knew him crucified him, and many in his time who didn't know him very well believed in him.

Ignorance of Scripture is ignorance of Jesus, said St. Jerome.

Our bearing and conversation should be such that, on seeing or hearing us, people will say, "This person thinks about the life of Christ!"

When the Christian believer asks what God is like, as the Apostle Philip did in today's Gospel (Jn 14:8), the answer is to look at the life and acts of Jesus. Jesus, as the early fathers of the Church called him, is the "great sacrament," who signifies who God is and what God does. That's the deep significance of what Jesus says when he tells the Apostles that if they had known him they would also have known the Father (v. 9).

Today's Gospel isn't the only time that Jesus made valuable promises to answer prayers of petition. He'd said in his Sermon on the Mount that if we ask it shall be given us, if we seek we shall find, if we knock the door will be opened to us (Mt 5:7f.). Later, he repeated his promise, saying that if two or more of us agree about anything for which we're to pray, it shall be granted (Mt 18:19). And at yet another time he said that whatever we ask for in prayer with faith, we will receive (Mt 21:22).

Jesus' words about prayer are reflected in the attitude of the anonymous poet, who wrote:

> I got up early one morning
> and rushed right into the day.
> I had so much to accomplish
> that I didn't have time to pray.
> Problems just tumbled about me,
> and heavier came each task.
> "Why doesn't God help me?" I wondered.
> He answered, "You didn't ask."
> I wanted to see joy and beauty.
> But the day toiled on, gray and bleak.
> I wondered why God didn't show me.
> He said, "But you didn't seek."
> I tried to come into God's presence;
> I tried all my keys at the lock.
> God gently and lovingly chided,

"'My child, you didn't knock."
I woke up early this morning,
and paused before entering the day;
I had so much to accomplish
That I had to take time to pray.

St. Paul meditated on Jesus often. Today's first reading relates that a good portion of the city of Antioch gathered to hear
the word of the Lord from him (v. 44). The common people's
widespread enthusiasm contrasted with the jealousy of the leaders (v. 45) at the success of himself and Barnabas in converting
non-Jews. Nevertheless, Paul and Barnabas continued to speak
fearlessly. Paul said that though *priority* of salvation was a privilege of the Jews, this didn't mean that salvation was *exclusively*
theirs (v. 46). So Paul and Barnabas went to the Gentiles — luck-
ily for us today!

In retaliation, some of the Jews stirred up a persecution
against them (v. 50). The way they did it was to approach faithful women, for whom at that time the Jewish religion had a special attraction because outside Judaism sexual morality was lax
and family life breaking down. The Jewish religion preached a
high level of morality.

By persuading the faithful women to have their husbands
(some of whom were in influential positions) take steps against
the Christian preachers, the leaders succeeded in having Paul and
Barnabas expelled from their territory. But even as the two
Apostles defiantly shook the dust of the town from their feet as
they departed (v. 51), they left disciples who were filled with joy
and the Holy Spirit (v. 52). With a zeal for spreading the name
of Jesus that should be a model for all of us, they traveled south-
east to Iconium.

The long and short of the Sacred Scriptures, tradition, and
history is that when we see Jesus we see God.

Holy Spirit, Companion and Teacher

There are various ways in which we can be present to each other. We can be present to each other on the telephone in one way, on TV in another way, as a speaker before an audience in yet another way, or face-to-face in a physical presence. Presence — especially the presence of friends — is important to us all, notably when lonely or troubled. At those times, to hear someone say words like, "I'm here for you," is balm for the soul.

In today's Gospel, the Apostles at the Last Supper were dejected because they were learning that Jesus' physical presence was to be no more. He assured them that his bodily presence would be replaced by something far more wonderful and no less intimate. From their having been able to physically see, hear, and touch him, they would now have his abiding presence through the indwelling of his Holy Spirit.

Judas, not the betrayer but the brother of James the Apostle, asked how it was possible that Jesus could manifest himself to them and not to the world. His question, along with other questions at various times from Apostles like Peter, Thomas, and Philip, show how imperfect was their understanding but how honest their inquiries.

The first part of Jesus' answer was that, whereas the world didn't love him, his followers were expected to. While the love of God for all the human race is a well-confirmed subject of both Testaments of the Bible, surprisingly the theme of people's *love* for Jesus isn't very common in the New Testament: the idea of *belief* in Jesus is more frequent. One of the few places where specific mention of love for Jesus occurs is in today's excerpt from St. John's Gospel. Jesus tells us clearly and directly how we're to show our love for him. Skip the moonlight and roses and pretty

poems: the best way to show love for him is to be true to his word
(v. 23).

The second part of Jesus' answer encouraged the Apostles
— and us — to seek enlightenment from the Holy Spirit. The
word which Jesus used for the Spirit was called in Greek, the
language in which St. John the Evangelist wrote, "Paraclete" (v.
26). As the poet (Gerard Manley Hopkins) put it, a paraclete is
one who cheers, who encourages, who persuades, who exhorts,
who stirs up, who urges forward. What clapping hands are to a
speaker, what a trumpet is to a soldier, the paraclete is to a soul.

The word "paraclete" is the equivalent of the Latin "advoca-
tus," and means a mediator, a defense attorney, one who stands
by you in time of need. In time of trouble, it's a great solace to
have a lawyer take your side. What the lawyer does for pay, the
Paraclete does for love. What the lawyer does with the possibility of failing, the Paraclete does with a guarantee of success for
those who do their part.

The word is also translated "comforter," but the Third Person of the Blessed Trinity does more than comfort. The Holy
Spirit is a presence of Jesus that's more intimate and personal and
vivid and convincing than anything merely intellectual. His presence flows primarily into love. This isn't something syrupy sweet
and sentimental. To avoid that, Jesus calls for our obedience. That
can at times call for what we today mean by the term "tough love."

The Holy Spirit was with Sts. Paul and Barnabas in the
events related in today's reading. They had been preaching for
some time in the synagogues at Iconium (about eighty miles east
of Antioch). Both Gentile and Jewish leaders there had threatened them, so they moved their activities to Lystra, about twenty
miles south.

In the pagan town of Lystra, Paul, seeing that a man who
had been crippled from birth had the faith to be cured, dramati-
cally told him to stand up. The man jumped up and began to walk
around. What kind of faith did the crippled man (v. 8) have?
Certainly not faith in Jesus Christ: these people worshipped many

gods. Yet Paul, guided by the Spirit, saw something of the core of the man. As with Jesus in his ministry, it wasn't the external trappings that were important, but what was in a person's soul.

The miracle caused the crowds, steeped in pagan mythology, to think that in the form of Paul and Barnabas the gods had come. For some reason they called Barnabas "Zeus," the chief of their gods, and Paul "Hermes," because he was the eloquent chief speaker. Even the priest of the temple of Zeus joined in the enthusiasm, bringing garlands of flowers to the temple and some oxen to be sacrificed in their honor. Their preparations for sacrifice were the first intimation that Paul and Barnabas had of what was afoot, because they hadn't understood the local peoples' dialect. Paul and Barnabas were horrified.

Paul then preached the first sermon in the New Testament addressed directly to non-Jews. These people were pagans, so he began with arguments from pure reason. For clues about the true nature of the living God, he referred not to the Scriptures but to nature and human experience: rains from heaven and fruitful seasons, nourishment and gladness (v. 17) — from what those people knew to what they didn't yet know. Even though his speech repudiated what they had stood for, the people remained enthusiastic.

Today, too, to help fill out our picture about God we turn to nature as well as the Scriptures. Unlike the pagans of Lystra, we've been taught the importance of the Holy Spirit. We, like the Apostles and Paul — and like Jesus himself — are to be obedient to the guidance of the Holy Spirit. The Holy Spirit sent Jesus forth on his ministry of world salvation, drawing him into desert nights of reflection, onto mountains of prayer, and into inspirations of teaching and healing. Paul expressed it in today's reading by telling us that God hasn't hidden himself without giving us a clue.

If the Holy Spirit's inspired word infuses our life, we will respond by springing up like the crippled man at Lystra.

Peace: God's Gift

Business seminars used to deal with what they called conflict resolution. Today, realizing that we don't really *resolve* many conflicts — human nature being what it is — they're more and more emphasizing the concept of conflict *management*. The major tactic is to try to give a full hearing to each side in a conflict and then see if each side can get what it wants without making the other side feel as though it has lost, and — most important — keeping peace.

Peace — external and internal — is vital for all of us. We commemorate external peace at special times like Memorial Day. Problems of internal peace such as undue anxiety and morbid scrupulosity we consider all the time. Jesus made peace an important part of his last lessons the night before he died. He said that he was giving us *his* gift of peace, "not as the world gives."

What the world means by "peace" is often simply the absence of war. By the Tiber River in Rome there is the glass-enclosed beautifully-carved marble *ara pacis,* "altar of peace." It was erected by Augustus Caesar after he and his armies had conquered practically all of Europe and the known parts of Asia. But when one bends others to one's will, that's not peace, but tyranny.

Or the world's peace is a state of being left alone, like what the harassed mother wants from her active young children or the worker wants from the public he's had to deal with for too long. Or it's not being burdened by cares or financial worries. Or it's a deep sleep, which is what the world understands when it writes "Rest in Peace" on its tombstones.

Among the differences between peace achieved through arms and the peace of Jesus Christ is that the peace of Christ has as its purpose to destroy enmity, not the enemy. Jesus' peace is a peace which is the fruit of victories, alright — but spiritual victories over oneself and not military ones over others. Jesus taught us that there's nothing to kill for, but there are things to die for.

Further, what Jesus means by the peace he pledged at the Last Supper is an active thing: a virtue, a state of mind, a disposition for benevolence. It contains certain prerequisites. If you want peace, you must have a still and quiet conscience, because there's no peace for the wicked (Is 48:22). If you want peace, you must work for justice. If you want peace, you must seek God's will. As Dante put over the doors of Paradise, "In His will is our peace." T.S. Eliot observed that if we do God's will we can find peace "even among these rocks" of our life. Jesus said that one of the essential requirements of peace is love.

Jesus wants his followers to have peace even in and with his departure. In fact, even in the face of his forthcoming departure, Jesus said, "if you loved me, you would rejoice" (v. 28). The importance of joy might escape us if we imagine that joy should invade us by itself, without our having to do anything to acquire it. This is, however, a mistake. Joy has to be pursued and conquered by a struggle against our evil tendencies, which are constant.

Usually a going away gift is for the person who is leaving. In today's Gospel, though, Jesus reverses that procedure and gives his disciples his farewell gift before his going away. And his gift is precious and practical — nothing less than peace. His kind of peace has nothing to do with only an end to psychological tension, or a sentimental feeling of well-being. It pertains to our salvation. And it's not a one-time-only present; whenever we celebrate the Eucharist we pray that God "grant us peace in our day." Then the presider and we pray for each other that "the peace of the Lord be with you always." We're not just peace-lovers, but peace-makers, peace-givers.

We offer each other a kiss of peace, a sign of the precious gift that Jesus wants to keep giving. We need a broad enough vision to see God's presence everywhere. At the head table in the cafeteria of a Catholic school, one of the nuns had placed a big bowl of bright red, fresh, juicy apples. Beside the bowl, she placed a note, which read, "Take only one. Remember, God is watching." At the other end of the table was a bowl full of freshly baked chocolate chip cookies, still warm from the oven. Beside that bowl was a little note scrawled in a child's handwriting which read, "Take all you want. God's watching the apples."

Part of seeing God everywhere is to recognize God's presence in every person. Michael and Patrick, brothers, were two of the most over-charged young boys in the elementary school. If ever there was a problem incident, both of them would be in the thick of it. One day, after one such "problem incident," Michael, the younger of the two, was told to report to the priest-principal's office.

The priest, sitting behind his desk, asked Michael to sit in a chair in front of the desk. Thinking it would help if he instilled an awareness of the presence of God, he quietly asked Michael, "Where is God?" Michael looked surprised and remained silent. The priest again asked him, this time more insistently, "Where is God?" Again Michael, appearing more frightened, remained silent.

For a third time, Father asked, "Where is God?" This time, though, he shouted it. Michael jumped out of the chair, bolted through the door, and ran all the way home. There, he told his brother Patrick, "Let's get packed and leave!" When Patrick asked why, Michael said, "They lost God and they're trying to blame it on us."

The "kiss of peace" at Mass is given in various ways beyond a simple embrace. An actual kiss can be the traditional caress with the lips in affection, greeting, and reverence. We may kiss our spouse on the mouth, a baby or others on the cheek, or officials on the hand as a ceremonial sign of homage. A kiss has always been held in awe. "The Kiss," a bronze sculpture made by Auguste Rodin in 1886, the most sensuous of his works, has sometimes been considered his masterpiece. A kiss is also a scene in one of the first moving pictures in the world, filmed by Thomas Edison in 1896, the first close-up of a screen embrace.

Or we may choose to extend our "kiss of peace" by a bow — a bending down as an expression of respect and salutation. Or we may offer our wish for peace by way of a handshake. But the handshake may be losing its grip. Some people want to eliminate it altogether: handshakes, they say, can transmit germs. Others counterargue that a handshake continues to create a degree of intimacy within a matter of seconds. Politicians who grab every hand they can on the campaign trail clearly believe this to be true.

Today's first reading gives an insight into how the Apostles' love for the Lord, now grown to a height it never achieved in the Gospels, gave them peace even through hardships.

In every city where Sts. Paul and Barnabas preached the word of God they were opposed by Jews. They had to organize the churches they founded in a way that made their survival possible. By the end of their first missionary journey of preaching the power of Easter, they had strengthened the disciples and exhorted them to persevere in the faith (v. 22). Their arduous but very successful journey established early Christianity.

We're now living in that new place that was built by the blood and love of Jesus and the first Apostles. In the midst of our hardships and disappointments, which are no greater than those faced by Jesus and the first Apostles, we must continue to rely upon the Lord's gift of his special peace.

Interior Life and Growth

To describe spiritual reality, in today's Gospel our Lord uses a figure that was familiar to the Jews: the figure of the vine and the branches. In a land where vineyards were as common as our fields of corn or wheat or potatoes, today's "true vine" comparison needed little explanation. Over and over the Jewish Scriptures pictured Israel as the vineyard of God, the people as branches of God's vine. The coins of the Maccabees had the symbol of the vine, and the Temple had a great golden vine carved into the front of its Holy Place. The vine is life-giving, full of vitality, and patiently cared for by God.

Jesus speaks of himself as the *true* vine, with us as his branches. Where does the vine end and where do the branches begin? Aren't they united? That's the way it's meant to be between Jesus and us. We receive our spiritual life of grace from our connection with him. Of ourselves we're as spiritually worthless as the cut-off branch of a vine, which is just about the most worthless of wood.

Lest we develop vices like pride, to bear abundant fruit we need pruning and trimming to be cut down to size. Some experts say that for every hundred people who can handle adversity, there's only one who can handle success. Only the humble can bear fruit in Christ. Jesus' benefit was his contact with the heavenly Father; ours is contact with God through Jesus.

This means dependence on God. Some people don't like to admit dependency. A little boy was afraid of the dark. One night his mother told him to go out to the back porch and bring her the broom. The boy said, "Mama, I don't want to go out there. It's dark." His mother smiled reassuringly at her son and said, "You don't have to be afraid of the dark. Jesus is out there. He'll protect you."

The boy asked, "Are you sure he's out there?" "Yes," she said. "I'm sure. He's everywhere, and he's always ready to help you when you need him."

The boy thought about that and went to the back door and cracked it a little. Peering into the darkness, he called, "Jesus? If you're out there, would you please hand me the broom?"

Even some people who acknowledge their dependence on other people sometimes don't like to admit dependence on God. That's one of the reasons for some of our world's mess. To sustain a sense of dependence on God — to be true branches — requires work. Branches have to be pruned and cared for, and the soil has to be watered, softened, and fertilized. If our spiritual life is to bear fruit, we have to work at enriching our souls by practices like reading, thinking, praying, and good conversation.

Only after cultivating our interior life and growth is proper *action* possible. What is proper action? Sometimes it may seem like *inaction*: As Milton said in his sonnet on his blindness: "They also serve who only stand and wait." People are accustomed to ask how much a person has *done*. They say little about the *virtue* one has cultivated: how poor in spirit he or she is, or how patient, how devout.

For the Jews, the sign of being on the vine was circumcision; through this mark, they reached back to Abraham (Gn 15). As with every religion, there are traditions and customs going back years. In order for non-Jews to be integrated into the Jewish faith, the Old Testament demanded faith in one God, circumcision, Jewish dress, and kosher food.

For St. Paul, however, the only requirement for entry into the Christian religion was faith in Christ and baptism. Paul went up to Jerusalem to engage in dialogue about an important issue. At that time, when most of those coming into the Christian Church were Jews, there was a controversy about whether it was necessary for a convert to Christianity to become a Jew first. Those who held that it was necessary to become a Jew first held to the necessity of circumcision for a man. They declared circumcision to be important to the Jews' bonds of love and loyalty to their God and one another.

That issue of circumcision was the first big controversy that rocked the early Church. The Apostles decided to convene a meeting in the year 50 A.D. which would become known as the Council of Jerusalem — the first ecumenical council (the last of which to date was Vatican Council II in 1962-65). The deliberations of that first council are read in the first readings of the Mass for the next few days.

What triumphed ultimately was the position espoused by Paul: that Jesus had brought the Old Law to its *fulfillment*. Because of Jesus' death and Resurrection, it was no longer necessary to be first a Jew in order to become a Christian. Not circumcision, but Jesus, is the source of Christian unity. He's the vine, we the branches.

Jesus makes us sharers in the very life of God! This new life is given, or is strengthened, particularly by means of the sacraments. In these seven efficacious means of grace we discover Jesus. There he speaks to us, there he forgives us, there he sanctifies us, there he offers us his reconciliation and friendship, there he gives us himself. Christians who break away from these connections to the vine are left without sufficient nourishment for their soul.

Thursday, Fifth Week of Easter
Ac 15:7-21; Jn 15:9-11

Believe, Love, and Be Happy

When a citizen of Sapanta, Romania, dies, a woodcarver carves a poetic and pictorial homage of the deceased onto an oak grave marker in what villagers now call the Merry Cemetery. The 800 or so carvings are on blue-painted oak slabs, decorated with floral borders and a riot of colors. This festival of color shows the dead either in life or when death caught them, while the simple poems are a final apologia for an often ordinary life. The pictures are rudimentary: of women spinning yarn, of farmers on prized tractors, a butcher with his cleaver in his hand and a pipe in his mouth, a teacher at his desk, a musician playing the local cello. Their epitaphs are conceived as a message from the dead person to the living world.

St. John's Gospel devotes over four of its twenty-one chapters to the last words of Jesus. Like other last words, they reflect the life and personality of the speaker. Jesus' farewell discourse is patterned upon that of the great Jewish leader Moses. Moses' last words stressed the importance of the commandments, and Jesus' last words alluded to his *new* commandment: love. Today's passage gives the way in which we can remain alive, grow, and be fruitful: that is, to remain in Jesus' love (v. 10).

We love what's good; *God's* love is what *makes* goodness. The truest, best, and most beautiful love in the world is God's. People wear dark glasses to accustom themselves to the sun's brightness. It's like that when we look at God's love. Human beings are called to imitate God's love. Modern medicine shows a connection between heart diseases and disorders in love.

The result of following his advice, says Jesus, will be joy (v. 11): *his unique* joy that will come our way, more fulfilling than any other and with a new completeness. There's a difference between joy and such things as happiness, beatitude, pleasure, and delight.

Happiness is the generic term — as we have when meeting a friend whom we haven't seen in years. Beatitude denotes intense happiness, usually with more elevated connotations — as what springs from purity of heart. Pleasure strongly implies a feeling of satisfaction, like an infant having food and warmth; it often implies positive gladness. Delight carries a stronger implication of liveliness in the satisfaction induced, often suggesting a less enduring emotion than pleasure, as we might have in reading a good novel or in eating a delicious meal.

Joy is often the preferred term when a deep-rooted, rapturous emotion is implied. Jesus' new and peerless joy that will come our way is more fulfilling than any other and with a new completeness. A joyless Christian is a contradiction in terms.

In today's passage from the Acts of the Apostles, we see an immediate exercise of what we call "tough love." Much of what Paul had been proposing about eating non-kosher food and indulging in other non-Jewish observances caused scandal to the Jews, even those who had become Christians. All of them were, after all, people of the Mosaic Law, and anything that was repugnant to them — for example, the eating of unbled meat and intermarriage among relatives — would have been scandalous.

Today's reading shows us St. Peter telling the other Apostles and the elders the decision about whether new converts to Christianity from both paganism and Judaism should be held to the Law of Moses. The long thought-out and prayed-over decision was that the Mosaic Law, as currently interpreted by the rabbis who had added countless restrictions, was not to be binding upon those coming into the Church.

That decision meant a break with Judaism. That was serious. After all, the Mosaic Law had been proclaimed in every town and read aloud on every Sabbath in every synagogue, as St. James said, and the Jews of the dispersion would find it hard to associate with those who didn't observe it strictly. Yet the initiative was God's, and the Church could only acknowledge and obey it. As Peter said, they weren't to challenge the manifest will of God.

At the suggestion of James, however, a certain sensitivity was expected — a respectful sensitivity that's always expected at all levels of the Church to each others' needs and differences! James substantiated his position with a Scripture quotation (Am 9:11f.). He qualified it with four minimal requirements for Jewish-Gentile co-existence based in Israel's "holiness code" (Lv 17-

18 [v. 20 here]). These four requirements were that new Christians abstain from anything contaminated by idols, from illicit sexual union, from the meat of strangled animals, and from eating blood. None of this means an absence of difficulties. But joy is one of the most irresistible powers in the world. It brings about calm; it soothes away anger, it wins people over. A cheerful person shows people what the presence of God can produce within the soul.

Jesus' Resurrection helps us to understand an even more intense pleasure and joy. We Christians evangelize and sanctify suffering, but not joy — at least not sufficiently. Young people — and not only they — are led to think of God as an enemy of joy, that with God all celebrations and every explosion of joy is a sin.

The themes of the Passion too often prevail over such Easter themes as exultation and celebration. Take, for example, the experience of a driver who one morning, was heading for San Francisco. As he rode up to a toll booth, he heard loud music. He looked around and saw that there were no sound trucks in the vicinity. Inside the toll booth, however, he saw the toll collector dancing.

"What are you doing?" he asked.

"I'm having a party," the attendant said.

"What about the rest of the collectors?" the driver said, as he looked at the other toll booths.

The attendant pointed down the row of toll booths and asked, "What do those look like to you?"

The driver said, "They look like... toll booths. What do they look like to you?"

He said, "Vertical coffins. At 8:30 every morning, live people get in them. Then they die for eight hours. At 4:30, like Lazarus raised from the dead, they reemerge and go home. For eight hours, their brain is on hold, and they're dead on the job, just going through the motions."

The driver was amazed. A row of people dead on the job,

and this one, in precisely the same situation, had figured out a way to live. The driver couldn't help asking the next question: "Why is it different for you? You seem to be having a good time."

He looked at the driver and said, "I knew you were going to ask that. I don't understand why anybody would think my job is boring. I have a corner office, glass on all sides. I can see the Golden Gate Bridge, San Francisco, and the Berkeley hills. Half the Western world vacations here — and I just stroll in every day and practice dancing."

Jesus' empty tomb is the assurance of the human aspiration for joy. The Resurrection of Christ is the supreme affirmation that at the end of life there's enjoyment. Jesus has broken the chain of pleasure that generates suffering, and has replaced it with the suffering that generates pleasure. So joy, not suffering, has the last word.

Friday, Fifth Week of Easter
Ac 15:22-31; Jn 15:12-17

The Commandment to Love

In the Church's First Ecumenical Council, the Council of Jerusalem, the Holy Spirit and the early Church Fathers decided not to lay on Christians any burden from the Law of Moses which wasn't strictly necessary. With that decision the Church was risking a wide-open debate. Being true peacemakers, the Church Fathers sent Judas (Barsabbas, not the Iscariot) and Silas to outposts to help the lukewarm to accept the decision. The Christian assembly had now officially broken ties with Judaism and arrived at a new step in defining itself.

The same principles of development are true of some Church regulations today, whose contents aren't doctrinal — like fish on Friday or vernacular languages in the liturgy. Up for discussion now could be items like the adaptation of Christianity to local culture in places like Africa and Asia, celibacy, women priests, biotechnology and human reproduction, cooperation with other religions, democracy in the Church, inter-religious dialogue, evangelization, bad politics, and the extent of the Vatican's responsibility to local churches.

The history of the Church has sordid pages (for some of which Pope John Paul II famously apologized) — the Crusades, the Inquisition, the immoral lives of some Renaissance Popes, Galileo — and is always in need of reform. But the Church is more than just a community of believers, although it is that; more than a people who study the Word of God and try to put it into their lives, although it is that; more than a people who share Sacraments, although it is that. The Church is an assembly guided by the Holy Spirit to teach Christ's truths authentically to every age.

Those truths don't change. There's no new Gospel. But Christ's Gospel has to be applied to new situations. There's nothing in the oak tree which wasn't first in the acorn, yet the oak has developed and changed. The Church continues to solve new problems as she has always done: by relying on the Holy Spirit. The Church remains a sure and absolute guide in matters of faith and morals. True and lasting harmony in the midst of changes in the Church can be achieved only in a context of love for all humankind.

In today's Gospel reading, Jesus gives us his unique command that we love one another as he has loved us (v. 12). Jesus had to remind us often of the need to love one another, because sometimes we act as though we're made for competition rather than cooperation and love.

Some time ago, at a Special Olympics, nine contestants, all physically or mentally disabled, assembled at the starting line for the 100-yard dash. At the gun, they all started out, not exactly in a dash, but with a relish to run the race to the finish and win.

All, that is, except one boy, who stumbled on the asphalt and began to cry. The other eight, hearing the boy, slowed down and looked. They all turned around and went back — every one of them. One girl with Down's Syndrome bent down, kissed him, and said, "This will make it better." Then all nine linked arms and walked across the finish line together. People who were there wept. Why? Because deep down we know that what matters most in this life is more than winning for ourselves. What truly matters is helping others win, even if it means slowing down and changing our course.

Jesus gave us the example of a love greater than any other. He laid down his life for us (v. 13). He calls all of us for whom he died *friends* (v. 14). Many people who kept on the straight and narrow through terrible temptations and were asked about how they did it, answered, "I had a friend." "How did you overcome alcoholism?" "I had a friend." "How did you withstand losing your job?" "I had a friend." "How did you survive your loss?" "I had a friend."

"Don't bug me! Hug me!" says the bumper sticker, recognizing the T-shirt axiom that hugs are fully returnable. One man who strongly believed this went around giving hugs to all sorts of people. Invited to come to a home for the disabled, he hugged people who were terminally ill, or severely retarded, or quadriplegic. Finally, he came to Leonard, who was wearing a big white bib, on which he was drooling. Overcoming his initial reluctance, the man took a deep breath, leaned down, and gave Leonard a hug. All of a sudden Leonard began to squeal, "Eeehh! Eeeeehh!" The man turned to the staff — physicians, nurses, orderlies — for some sort of explanation, only to find that every one of them was crying. To his inquiry, "What's going on?" the head nurse said, "This is the first time in 23 years we've ever seen Leonard smile." It was because of outgoing love rather than routine care.

Our neighbors in need may be suffering for different reasons: loneliness, perhaps, or lack of love or abandonment. Their needs may be of the body — hunger, clothing, shelter, employment. Perhaps they're suffering the grave wound of ignorance. Maybe their hurt is the moral wound of sin which can be cured by the Sacrament of Penance.

Among the works showing love to our neighbor, very important are advice, counsel, support, pardon, edification — and patience. We live in an impatient age trying to make everything and everyone around us move faster — faster computers, faster Internet access, faster microwave ovens, faster trains, faster bicycles, faster cars. And there are many things that try the offshoot of love called patience: traffic jams, offensive drivers, incompetent sales clerks, repair workers who don't come when they say they will, long lines, computer glitches, gadgets that don't work. Patience allows us to take others' foibles and annoyances in stride — perhaps even to find them amusing. Patience is also the essence of civility, diplomacy, lawfulness, and civil order. Without it, society can't function.

Becoming more patient can help us be more effective, less overwhelmed, less angry, kinder, more tolerant, more loving — and also more lovable. We start cultivating patience by remembering that each person is different. No one sees and does things exactly as we do. We have to remind ourselves often that the world isn't all about concern for us, but rather that we're part of a much larger community with different interests and styles.

Often all that's necessary for love is a smile, a word of encouragement, the willingness to bite one's tongue in the face of an insult, visiting a friend who is sick or lonely, the exercise of such social virtues as warm greetings and words of thanks. Of course, social virtues have to be taught. A second-grader came up to Sister's desk and said, "I have to go to the bathroom." Sister corrected him in a whisper, "May I please go to the bathroom?" "Oh, do you have to go, too?" he asked. Certain professions, as health care and social work, are a continual work of mercy.

Whenever we find another human being in need, let's realize that we've found something more valuable than money — the opportunity to show love by caring for another.

Ac 16:1-10; Jn 15:18-21

Do You Belong to the World?

Jesus, whom we've been hearing this week speaking eloquently at the Last Supper about love, now makes a 180-degree turn to the opposite side of the circle of relationships. Now he speaks of hate. This is the hate which the world has for him and for all who take up his values. We found earlier a sharp division between the disciples of Jesus and the world which won't receive him, and now the dualism of that imagery rises to a new pitch.

In the New Testament, the word "world" is ambiguous. It can refer to what Jesus came to save, and is thus good, or to the realm of darkness as opposed to the realm of God's light. That's true also of St. John's Gospel, an excerpt of which we have here. In John's writings (as well as St. Paul's) "the world" is good because it's the possession of Christ by virtue of its very creation by God, and also through Jesus' redemptive sacrifice for it.

Today's passage, however, is a part of John's Gospel that presents Jesus and his disciples as more and more in opposition to the prince of this world and his followers (Jn 12:31). This aspect of the world hates Jesus (Jn 7:7). The nonbelieving Jews are of this world, but Jesus isn't (Jn 8:23). Jesus has come to judge "the world" (Jn 9:39; 12:31). The sin of "the world" and the cause of its rejection is its refusal to believe in the Son of God (Jn 8:44f.; 9:39-41; 16:9).

Today's passage shows the human being as caught between the two realms. The idea that good triumphs over evil is here. But the cost of that victory can be high. We have to make up our minds about whether we sign up for the pettiness of this world and its limits or whether we're traveling toward the domain of God which offers us so much more.

The world will hate the disciples as it did Jesus, because his disciples are now the agents whom he's sending. As this theme is repeated, we're constantly reminded of the hostile exchanges between Jesus and the leaders of the Jews. The sin which the world incurs in persecuting Jesus' disciples is the same hatred that was demonstrated in its treatment of Jesus.

In our day, however, the "world" has learned that ennui may be more effective in opposing Christian principles than outright expressions of hatred. Nevertheless, Jesus' words today are a reminder that there has always been and always will be a countercultural aspect about the authentic Christian character.

The life of St. Paul is a demonstration of that. During the period in which St. Luke wrote his Acts of the Apostles, the Christian Church was growing; it needed assistants, and new communities needed to be formed. In the time of today's passage, Paul was on his second missionary journey. Timothy, whom Paul met in Lystra, was the son of a Jewish mother, Eunice, and a Gentile father. Such mixed marriages were, according to the Law of Moses (Dt 7:3), illegal. But if they took place and the mother was Jewish, the Jewish religion considered her offspring to be Jewish.

According to the Jewish religion, Timothy should have been circumcised in infancy. But he wasn't. So Paul, now exercising his office of rabbi, circumcised him according to the Jewish rite. For a grown man like Timothy, this was very painful. But this would help Timothy's ministry to be accepted by Christian believers who had been Jews.

Paul's surprising circumcision of Timothy gives rise to questions. Did it suggest loyalty to the Mosaic Law as binding upon Jews who had become Christian? Or did it give evidence of Paul's missionary ideal of being all things to all people (1 Cor 9:20-22)? Timothy had already been baptized, and Paul could certainly not have compromised the stand he consistently took against the Judaizers (Gal 5:2f.), even to win converts. The Judaizers wanted Christian converts from Judaism to adopt the customs, beliefs, and characteristics of Judaism. Luke's mention of the event serves his intense concern to show Paul standing squarely within observant Judaism, rigorously faithful to the Torah, and thus forging the continuity between Israel and Christianity.

Paul's vision at night (v. 9) is the first of five visions of Paul in Luke's accounts. Like other venerated figures, Paul received instruction and encouragement from heaven in dreams that preceded momentous stages of his mission, especially in dangers so great as to put its successful completion in doubt. The Macedonian man who stood before him represented the new non-Jewish audience whom Paul was being hastily propelled to evangelize. The vision assured success despite all hazards.

How far are we willing to go with the world? How far do we bravely participate in the Lord's ministry?

Monday, Sixth Week of Easter
Ac 16:11-15; Jn 15:26-16:4

Witnessing to Jesus

Everybody knows by now — from TV if nowhere else — that in our legal system, circumstantial evidence isn't the best way to establish the truth or falsity of an allegation. What is needed are reliable, trustworthy, believable witnesses.

In today's Gospel, Jesus said that his two major witnesses are the Paraclete — the Holy Spirit — and each one of us. It's an awesome responsibility that Jesus would depend on us to tell "the truth, the whole truth, and nothing but the truth" about his saving, loving words and works.

We're not usually called upon, of course, to witness for Jesus in the context of a courtroom. Our witnessing is rather the day by day dedication we give by our life as loyal Christians — the way we work and pray and play. And we don't witness alone: we have the help of the Holy Spirit. In fact, these are days for us to prepare for our celebration of the solemn coming of the Holy Spirit to the Church in a special way at Pentecost, which we shall be celebrating in less than two weeks.

The Holy Spirit wants to give us His gifts in such abundance that they form a torrential river in our spiritual life. He's waiting for us only to rid our souls of possible obstacles, to ask for greater purification, and to tell Him from the depth of our soul that we want Him to come and fill the hearts of His faithful and enkindle in them the fire of His love.

The torrent of God's grace comes to us in what are known as the gifts of the Holy Spirit. Traditionally, these gifts are seven. The gift of *understanding* shows us with great clarity the riches of the faith. The gift of *knowledge* enables us to judge created things in an honest way, and to keep our heart fixed on God and on things insofar as they lead to Him. The gift of *wisdom* enables us to comprehend more of the unfathomable wonder of God and to seek Him in preference to everything else. The gift of *counsel* points out the paths of holiness — God's will in daily life — and encourages us to choose the option which most closely coincides with the glory of God and the good of people. The gift of *piety* inclines us to approach God with the intimacy with which a child approaches his father. The gift of *fortitude* lifts us up continually, helping us to overcome inevitable difficulties. The gift of *fear* induces us to flee the occasions of sin, resist temptation, avoid every evil which could sadden the Holy Spirit, and above all to avoid the loss of the One who is the reason of our being.

Today's passage from the Acts of the Apostles shows how the Gospel was spreading, and will eventually lead St. Paul to the center of the Empire: Rome. First, though, we find him here in a leading city, Philippi, which had an industry in fine cloths. Lydia met the criteria for Church membership laid down early on, including a respect for God and an openness to God's word.

Today's excerpt also helps to correct the misconception of Paul's being anti-feminist. Paul, when he had persecuted Christians, hadn't discriminated against women: he had dragged off both women and men. Now, too, he didn't discriminate against participation by women in the spread of the Gospel. If he had been as fiercely anti-feminist as alleged in some quarters, a woman as sophisticated and discerning as Lydia, a wealthy woman who graciously offered him the use of her home as his headquarters, would not have been won to Christianity by Paul's preaching.

This good woman was in the tradition of many other good women in the New Testament: the women who ministered to Jesus in his ministry, the Samaritan woman at the well who brought the first news of Jesus the Redeemer to her townsfolk (Jn 4:39), Priscilla and Chloe of Corinth, Phoebe of Cenchreae, the mother of Rufus who cared for Paul as if he were her own son, the daughters of Philip of Caesarea, and many other women who made enormous contributions to the life of the Church. This passage shows us, too, that women can be great witnesses. In fact, women are the stronger sex. Men in the United States typically die almost six years before women do. By the age of 100, women outnumber men eight to one.

The superiority of women can be illustrated by a humorous story. A patient's family gathered to hear what the specialists had to say. "Things don't look good," said the doctor in charge, "the only chance is a brain transplant. This is an experimental procedure. It might work, but the bad news is that brains are very expensive, and you will have to bear the costs yourselves."

"Well, how much does a brain cost?" asked the relatives.

"For a male brain, $500,000. For a female brain, $200,000."

The patient's daughter wasn't satisfied, and asked, "Why the difference in price between male brains and female brains?"

"A standard pricing practice," said the head of the team. "You see, women's brains have to be marked down because they've actually been used."

We witness to the Lord according to our given nature, talents, and qualities. Women's nature, often more than that of men, has a gentle warmth, an untiring generosity, an ability with detail, intuitiveness, simple and deep piety, and constancy.

Today we ask the Holy Spirit to bend all our stubborn hearts and wills, to melt the frozen, to warm the lukewarm in dealing with God, and to guide the steps that go astray (Sequence of the Mass of Pentecost).

Tuesday, Sixth Week of Easter
Ac 16:22-34; Jn 16:5-11

God's Paraclete

"What's in a name?" Shakespeare's Juliet asked, and we agree with her that any other name than "rose" wouldn't diminish the flower's fragrance. Today, the principle seems to be "If it's unpopular, just rename it." Because people are worried about the vulnerability of nuclear power plants, the industry has begun to rename them "energy centers." Years ago, used cars were called "pre-owned"; now they're "previously enjoyed" cars. The unattractive word "gambling" has given way to the elegant-sounding "gaming." Since the word "vouchers" tests poorly in polls, parents who want to send their children to other than government schools use "school choice"; this irritates those who favor every conceivable use of the word "choice" except for "school choice." "Nontraditional sexuality" refers to sexual practices that are criminal or likely to put large numbers of people into shock.

Several times in our recent liturgies we've heard a name which may have caused us to wonder, "What's in *that* name?" The name is "Paraclete" (v. 7). God's love caused Jesus to promise to give us the Third Person of the Godhead in order to help give God's peace to us upon his physical departure. The Paraclete must guide Jesus' community, because Jesus hadn't been able to tell his disciples everything they had to know, and they weren't able to understand all his words and actions prior to his glorification.

Paracletes take place on a human as well as a divine level. When the heartbroken Nathaniel Hawthorne went home to tell his wife that he was a failure and had been fired from his job in a customhouse, she surprised him with an exclamation of joy!

"Now," she said triumphantly, "you can write your book!"

"Yes," replied Nathaniel, "and what shall we live on while I'm writing it?"

To his amazement, she opened a drawer and pulled out a substantial amount of money. "Where on earth did you get that?" he exclaimed.

"I've always known that someday you would write a masterpiece," she told him. "So every week, out of the housekeeping money you gave me, I saved a little. So here's enough to last us for a whole year!"

From her confidence and encouragement came one of the great novels of United States literature, *The Scarlet Letter*.

In our everyday life, a child falls down and skins a knee, and immediately runs to a parent for comfort. The injury continues to hurt, but now the child is no longer alone, and is comforted. Adults, too, have a need to be helped by someone willing to join in the trying experiences of life. Perhaps we experienced the urgency at a time of serious illness, or at the death of someone close, or when we were so desperate that we didn't know where to turn, or we were being lied about or ridiculed, or were in need of a job or money. In these human situations we experience the ache for someone who will help.

On the spiritual level, we ache for the power and comfort of the Holy Spirit. The Holy Spirit — the best gift in love God can give — stands beside us, comforts us when we ask, and helps us in difficult times. Although even people with no religious faith can comfort one another, our fellowship with the Holy Spirit of

God is deeper and more awesome. That doesn't mean ecstatic speech or luminous visions. The Holy Spirit is most often more quiet — and more available — than some people believe. All spiritual life, all holiness comes from the Father through Jesus by the action of the Holy Spirit.

From time to time, if we have the sensitivity to perceive it, we're aware of what's happening as we share the Holy Spirit with one another. The Spirit is present in even little actions: our common kindnesses, loving concern, and bursts of inspiration. Sometimes, though, we're fearful of those touching experiences, not knowing how to handle the emotion that often surrounds them. In other words, we sometimes give the Spirit of God a difficult time in his attempts at breaking through.

We are mindful of Jesus' words that the functions of the Holy Spirit are judicial. Although, as we've said, "Paraclete" usually suggests an advocate or defender, here He's turned into Israel's accuser. He will expose sin as well as righteousness for what they are (v. 8). In these juridical terms, the legal suit of Jesus against the world is decided in Jesus' favor. The sin of which the world is convicted is the "unbelief" throughout the Gospel. Because Jesus is returning to his heavenly Father, he's proved to be God's agent, and the "righteousness" of those who condemned him is proved to be false. The "ruler" of this world is also condemned. Those who seek to kill Jesus are doing the works of their father, the devil.

Today's first reading displays the Holy Spirit of God at work in the early Church. St. Paul's peaceful life at Philippi was suddenly shattered. Paul and his current companion in prison, Silas, were praying and singing hymns to God when a severe earthquake broke down the prison gates. Paul and Silas could have escaped, but didn't. That calm strength didn't penetrate the jailer, however. He woke up, saw the prison gates wide open, realized that he would be held responsible for his prisoners' escape, and drew his sword to kill himself. Paul yelled for him not to harm himself and, to make a long story short, baptized the jailer and his entire household. It wasn't just the decision of the prisoners not to run away that transformed a panicked jailer into a steady man: It was faith that made the difference.

We, too, possess hidden resources of strength, if our faith is so strong that we truly believe in Jesus' love and power to save us. Just as the jailer prepared a celebratory meal with his entire household to celebrate his conversion, in the Eucharist we dine with the living saints and with the souls beyond the grave.

Wednesday, Sixth Week of Easter
Ac 17:15, 22-18:1; Jn 16:12-15

Being Led to *Complete* Truth

In our time we consider a sneeze as being usually a symptom of an allergy or a common cold and nothing to be especially scared of (except as the possible spreader of germs). That was not always so. In biblical times, a sneeze was regarded as a sign of great personal danger. Possibly because sneezing had been a frequent occurrence during the great Athenian plague in classical Greece, people there assumed it was the first indication that a person had a dreaded disease. Ancient Romans saw in it an evil omen; some felt that the sneeze indicated the threatening presence of evil spirits.

The ancient Hebrews believed that a person who sneezed was near death. The fear was based on an erroneous but widely-held notion. A person's soul was considered to be the essence of life. The fact that dead people didn't breathe led to the deduction that the soul must be breath. This was supported by the biblical story that God, when creating the first man, "breathed into his nostrils the breath of life." If air were the substance of the soul and so much of it left suddenly through a sneeze, wasn't it likely that, for a person deprived of this essence of life, death might be inevitable?

It's thus not surprising that from the earliest days people learned to respond to a sneeze with apprehension and the fervent wish to the sneezer that God may bless him to preserve his life. The medieval Pope Gregory the Great introduced the saying, "God bless you," to anyone who sneezed. During his reign the Roman population was decimated by a plague believed to have been caused by contamination of the air. This, it was thought, made people who sneezed "give up the ghost" immediately.

The ancient viewpoints had this much in common: the very word for "spirit" in Hebrew, Greek, and Latin is the same as the word for "breath" and "life." The idea can be applied to the Holy Spirit, the Third Person of the Blessed Trinity. Today's reading from St. John's Gospel shows Jesus at the portion of his Last Supper where he highlighted the Holy Spirit. The Holy Spirit represents the continued presence of God, sustaining Jesus' followers, clarifying his message, and bringing a fuller understanding of God's revelation. Although the Holy Spirit is called many things — the Paraclete, the Advocate, Intercessor, Consoler, Comforter — here Jesus emphasized the Holy Spirit's role of abiding guidance: to lead the disciples to a fuller understanding of Jesus, to free us, give us a sense of direction, enable us to understand Jesus as "the way, the truth, and the life."

Jesus speaks of the Holy Spirit of truth who will guide us to all truth. Because "all truth" can only be found in the impenetrably mysterious God, we see the mind-boggling scope of the task.

We've come to recognize the Holy Spirit in three aspects. First, as participant in creation — when, as the Book of Genesis beautifully portrays (1:2), the Spirit of God moved upon the face of the waters, bringing order out of chaos. Secondly, God's Holy Spirit prepares the world for redemption through Jesus' life, ministry, teaching, and sacrifice. Thirdly, He has guided, and still guides, humankind into all truth, inspiring us to acts restraining evil, promoting good, and leading us onward to union with God.

A contrast with Jesus' joyful promise in the Gospel is St. Paul's failure in today's reading from the Acts of the Apostles. Paul found himself among the Greeks of ancient Athens, then the most famous city in the Greek world. Prominent philosophers conducted their discussions there. Paul wanted to engage them in dialogue. But he had little street credibility.

In an encounter between the word of God and the whole of the Greek world — the world of culture of the time — Paul stood on the Areopagus, that impressive spot where the Athenians' supreme tribunal used to meet, at the upper city committed to the gods. Paul saw at the Areopagus the beauty of the bodies carved out of marble in the Pantheon, the temple dedicated to all the gods there. The ancient Greeks reveled in the perfect expression of the human form; they carved some of the most exquisite statues of male and female which still remain among the wonders of the world.

Among their altars to their many gods, they had one dedicated to the "Unknown God." Paul directed the attention of his listeners to that one. He went on to tell them that what they were worshiping in ignorance he would make known to them. His speech was well-prepared, polished, well-articulated, and carefully reasoned — as he knew the highly-educated Athenians would require. He referred to Jesus as one whose approval by God was shown by God's having raised him from the dead.

Paul drew a picture of God using their terminology. Perhaps he relied too much on human artifice, too little on the Holy Spirit. Some Athenians sneered, while others condescendingly put him off by saying they would listen to him at some other time.

For quite some time after leaving Athens for Corinth he felt that failure keenly. It seemed that the Athenians were partial to new discourses, then paid them no mind. They were interested only in having something new to talk about. Nevertheless, Paul's preaching in Athens gave rise to the first Christian community there. Among those who came to believe were Dionysius the Areopagite and a woman named Damaris.

People who announce Jesus today must, first of all, rely upon the Holy Spirit. Then we must be willing, like Paul, to be unpopular at times, forgoing success in human terms, and accepting the more demanding aspects of Jesus' teaching — mortification, honesty in business and professional matters, fidelity to family life, chastity in and outside marriage. There's no other prescription for curing our sick world.

Thursday, Sixth Week of Easter
Ac 18:1-8; Jn 16:16-20

Sorrow Turned into Joy

During World War II, eight thousand paratroopers of the First British Airborne Division landed in Arnhem, Holland, behind the German lines in September 1944, and held the area for nine days and nights, with a loss of six thousand men. In a speech before the House of Commons, Winston Churchill said: "'Not in Vain' may be the pride of those who survived and the epitaph of those who fell." The poet Robert Frost suggested for his own epitaph, "I had a lover's quarrel with the world." An appropriate epitaph for any Christian might read: "To be continued."

If your epitaph were being written today, how would it read? What would it say about you? Would it announce that you touched the world in a positive way, or would it be blank? You may not think of it often, but your epitaph really is being written today — and by you.

Jesus' farewell discourse is patterned upon that of the great Jewish leader Moses. Today's Gospel is part of it. St. John's Gospel devotes over four of its twenty-one chapters to the last words of Jesus.

Jesus referred to the fact that he was to be taken up into heaven. This doesn't mean that his ascent was elevator-like. Heaven isn't up, hell isn't down. The idea that heaven is up and hell down started with the ancients' view of the cosmos. Their view was that over the flat earth was a solid vault of sky, above which was God's throne. Heaven was *up*: somewhere in the great beyond. For them, it was necessary for Jesus to go "up there," either by simply vanishing or by some kind of visible ascension. We, on the other hand, regard heaven as a state of blessedness with God in a place that's cosmologically undeterminable.

The atheist Soviet leader Nikita Khrushchev once ridiculed Christianity by remarking that his cosmonauts, on their journeys in space, had never reported seeing Jesus passing by. What he in his poor humor didn't know is that all stories about outer space, including that of Jesus' Ascension, are based on cosmological assumptions of a particular time and place.

The movement of Jesus' Ascension isn't from the ground up into the clouds, but from the human place to the divine place. Jesus' expression that he was going back to the Father symbolizes Jesus' close relationship to God and his role as God's agent. All together this "Good News" is cosmic: Jesus' life, death, Resurrection, and Ascension affect not only human beings, but the whole universe. Like impatient children in the back seat of the car who badger their parents with their incessant, "Are we there yet?," Jesus' disciples wanted him to clarify his comment in terms more specific than "a short time" for his Second Coming. Was it to be days? weeks? months? years? decades? centuries? millennia? Jesus didn't satisfy their curiosity. He added solid advice: be watchful!

Through his Resurrection and Ascension Jesus would cease to be present in his Church in one way in order to be present in another — a way that's more profound and intimate. There had to be one final moment when Jesus entered the fullness of glory that was his. His Resurrection appearances couldn't go on forever. And they couldn't just taper off; their end had to be specific, definitive.

We now have the living and lasting presence of him who at his birth was called "Emmanuel" — "God with us." Jesus, the living head of his body the Church, remains always with us as he promised. His presence with us can make our earth, our daily life, a heaven. He's with us when we gather, two or three, in his name. He's with us in the proclamation of his word and in the sharing of bread and wine. He's with us in saving those who approach the heavenly Father through him.

The work of God after Jesus began with the deeds of the Apostles. Today's first reading tells us about some of this. After his failure in cultured Athens, St. Paul left for the very different Corinth, the main port of Greece, noted not for culture but for commerce and wealth, and famous for the worship of Aphrodite, the goddess of love, who in Rome became the goddess Venus, the worship of whom involved sexual excesses.

It must have been a great comfort for Paul to meet with Aquila and his wife Priscilla, who shared the same trade of tentmaking as himself and kindly put themselves at his service — an example of true hospitality. They were converts to Christianity whose home became a Christian meeting place. The Emperor Claudius had issued a short-lived edict ordering all Jews to leave Rome because of their fighting among themselves, probably over the messiahship of Jesus; the Roman authorities classed both factions — those who followed Jesus and those who rejected him — simply as Jews.

While Paul was absorbed in preaching at Corinth, Silas and Timothy came down from Macedonia with a report from up north in Thessalonica. In general, the condition of the Church there was favorable, but some of the Thessalonian Christians had misunderstood the *Parousia*, Jesus' Second Coming. Because some people thought it imminent, they did no work; some gave in to immorality; some were perplexed over the fate of the dead, believing that their friends and relatives who died before Jesus' *Parousia* would be at a disadvantage. Paul would try to straighten them out with two letters. The preliminary picture of confusion eventually gave way to an awareness that was from God.

God always knows the depth of our confusion. His saving presence continues to work in us. In this season of Easter joy, it's up to us to keep *all* of Jesus in mind: his life, his last words, his death, Resurrection, and Ascension, as a suitably accurate and inspiring epitaph.

Friday, Sixth Week of Easter
Ac 18:9-18; Jn 16:20-23

Seeing Life as Sad and Glad

On one of his radio shows, the comic Jack Benny, who had built a fictitious reputation as the cheapest man in the world, was stopped by a thief who threatened, "Your money or your life!" There followed a lengthening silence, and in due course the audience, catching on, began to laugh louder and louder. When the laughter finally died down, the thief said, "Come on, your money or your life!" To which Jack Benny replied querulously, "I'm *thinking!* I'm *thinking!*"

Our whole lives consist of sadness and joy. Jesus recognizes this when he speaks in his Last Supper discourses of his disciples being sad for a time and of their grief turning into joy. His comparison with the pregnant woman who is in pain during labor but joyful when she's given birth to a son had been applied to the expectation of the messianic age in the Old Testament — for example, the "birth pangs" of Zion (Is 66:7-10). Birth pangs can also refer to the trials faced by the faithful in the last days.

We have the promise of the kingdom in our lives and in our world. But building the kingdom isn't like building a sky-scraper, where there's an end point and joy about completion. We're dealing with human beings, free will, and grace. Only at the end will we see how everything fits together.

So it's comforting to know that, according to Jesus in today's Gospel, gladness, not sadness, has the last word. Jesus overcame the sadness of his death with the limitless gladness of his Resurrection. Because it's the risen Jesus who abides with us, the true source of our gladness is always with us.

To comprehend it all, God sends the Holy Spirit (whose arrival on the scene we celebrate soon, at Pentecost), who in turn gives us many spiritual gifts, one of which is understanding. Through this gift, which is necessary for living a fully Christian life, we come to a deeper knowledge of the mysteries of faith. Under this light supernatural truths give an indescribable joy which is a foretaste of heaven. Thanks to this gift, says St. Thomas, God Himself is glimpsed here below.

The Holy Spirit's gifts can enable us to grasp the deeper meaning of the Scriptures, the life of grace, and the presence of Jesus in each Sacrament, especially the Eucharist. For the eyes of Jesus' faithful, there's a whole new universe to be discovered. The divine secrets of the Blessed Trinity, the Incarnation, the Redemption, and the Church can become living realities affecting our day-to-day life. These inscrutables can come to have a decisive influence on how we live, what we do at work, how we conduct our family life, and how we deal with friendships. Those who are docile to the Holy Spirit become purified in soul, are awakened in faith, and can discover God in everyday events.

We will receive the gift of understanding in the measure in which we respond to grace, are pure of heart, and strive earnestly for personal holiness. The way to achieve the *fullness* of this gift is by personal prayer in which we contemplate the truths of faith;

by a joyful, loving struggle to maintain the presence of God throughout the day; and by fostering contrition whenever we have cut ourselves off from God. The soul then makes discoveries about the supernatural, as it were like a little child opening his eyes to the world around him.

When St. Paul was in Corinth, he appreciated the truth of these insights through both his prayers and the way he lived his life for the Lord after his conversion. His dream-vision of the exalted Lord is a carefully planned intensification of his actions up to their culmination in his victory before the Roman proconsul Gallio. God's assurances in Paul's vision make intelligible the extended sojourn of a year and a half (A.D. 51-52) in the city of Corinth amid vigorous opposition. He was involved in both the promise and the pain involved in giving birth to the kingdom.

Today's first reading tells how Paul was brought before the tribunal of Gallio (elder brother of the philosopher Seneca). The story has strong local color and elements of burlesque. The Jews' charge that Paul was acting contrary to the law (v. 13) deliberately left open the question of whose law had been violated, the law of Rome or the Law of Moses. The proconsul wasn't misled. Preempting Paul's self-defense, he ruled in a way that was exemplary for public officials involved in controversies between Jews and Christians: Gallio's concern wasn't religious law but wrongdoing against the state (v. 14). And of wrongdoing against the state this Christian preacher couldn't be accused.

Paul experienced the sadness of seeing the Gentile crowd in full view of Gallio beat the Jew Sosthenes (v. 17), a leading man of the synagogue who had favored Paul. Gallio wasn't concerned. Happily, however, Paul's mission to Corinth was successful.

All of this took place toward the end of Paul's sojourn in the city (v. 18). A rapid travelogue brings us back to Syria via Ephesus, and abruptly Paul was back in Asia. The account of each stop is brief. Paul had his hair cut at Cenchreae, seaport of Corinth. He had made a Nazarite vow to serve God for a time.

During the time of his consecration to this vow, one of the things not permitted was the cutting of one's hair. At the end of this time, though, one of the things he had to do was have his hair cut and throw the hair into the flames on the altar according to Temple ritual (Nb 6:1-21).

Laughter and sorrow are as closely commingled in our lives as Siamese twins. They must be in equilibrium. Madness comes when one overtips the other, turning a mood into an entire mode of being. The person who's funny all the time isn't funny at all. Holy laughter, Dante claimed, is one of the special gifts of Paradise. Those who reject it reject God Himself. That's why Thomas More, soon to be murdered by King Henry VIII, comforted his friends with the assurance that before long they would be reunited "merrily in heaven."

We can't avoid some pain in our lives, but through the sadness we should never forget the Lord's promise to make us glad. The gladness is more a part of Christianity than the sadness.

Saturday, Sixth Week of Easter

Ac 18:23 28; Jn 16:23-28

Whom the Heavenly Father Loves

The two horrendous airplane crashes into the World Trade Center in New York City on September 11, 2001, killed almost three thousand people. Many people asked, "Where was God?", but some wrote about God's presence there. God was, one person said, on the one-hundred-and-tenth floor in a smoke-filled room with a man who called his wife to say "good-bye." God held the man's fingers steady as he dialed. He gave him the peace to say, "Honey, I'm not going to make it, but it's okay. I'm ready to go."

He was with that man's wife when he called as she was feeding their children. God held her up as she tried to understand her husband's words.

God was at the base of the building with the priest ministering to the injured and devastated souls. He took that priest home to tend to his flock in heaven. God was on those planes, in every seat, with every prayer. He was with the crew as they were overtaken. God saw every face, knew every name — though not all knew Him. Some sought Him with their last breath. Some couldn't hear Him calling to them through the smoke and flames. Some chose, for the final time, to ignore Him.

To many, even faithful believers, the promise Jesus makes in today's Gospel — that whatever we ask the Father He will give us — seems preposterous. God often seems absent when we need Him most.

Whatever we ask our heavenly Father in Jesus' name, the Savior tells us, He will give us. The prayer of petition has two aspects: the recognition that the mystery of God can't be put under human control, and the awareness we have from experience that what we request is often not granted as requested: we ask for one thing, get another. So the prayer of petition must take the form of surrendering oneself to the God of mystery whose care we seek. Disciples will know what to ask of the Father, and He won't refuse them. They will also be able to discern what God doesn't want.

Jesus gave us in Gethsemane the best example of how to make our prayer of petition — that we see God's will in His answer to our request. It was not the heavenly Father's will for Jesus to be relieved of his coming suffering and death, as Jesus requested. But Jesus had asked that the heavenly Father's will be done (Lk 22:42). The heavenly Father didn't prevent Jesus' sufferings and death, but amazingly answered Jesus' petition — with the Resurrection!

Equally amazingly, at this of all times — the Last Supper — Jesus said (v. 24) that if his disciples asked the heavenly Fa-

ther in his name their *joy* would be full. The fullness of joy is to
be had in God alone. This will prove true even in the persecu-
tions his disciples would suffer. At the coming of the Paraclete
at the first Pentecost, Jesus' disciples would finally understand
what was as yet clouded. But now, even the night before he died,
the Apostles, not yet enlightened by the Holy Spirit, hardly understood many of our Lord's sayings. He had often deliberately
spoken in veiled language. As Jesus' glorification approached, the
stories which he had used to illustrate divine truths would be
made clearer. The Apostles' new relationship with the heavenly
Father would enable them to approach Him confidently in prayer
as Jesus had. Jesus had come from the heavenly Father and would
return to Him. His disciples will be rewarded through the love
the Father has for those who love His Son.

Among these was Saul of Tarsus, who would become the
great St. Paul. In today's reading from the Acts of the Apostles,
he was at Ephesus, on his third missionary journey. From there
he sent his Letter to the Galatians and his First Letter to the
Corinthians, and continued his mission of strengthening the disciples in places like Galatia and Phrygia (Ac 18:23). Meanwhile
the faithful continued to build up the Church in Ephesus with
the help of Apollos, who with his gift of eloquent speech and
knowledge of the Sacred Scriptures (v. 24) had become a valued
missionary.

Initially, Apollos knew only a little of Christianity. Although
he was already preaching about the way of the Lord, that was
because he had been a follower of John the Baptist (v. 25), whose
preaching had reached Ephesus before the teaching about Jesus
did. (This shows how strong and widespread was the influence
of John the Baptist.) Some of the Baptist's disciples, in an immature Christianity, were giving a messianic acclaim to Apollos
which should have been reserved for Jesus.

So Apollos had to be set straight by Aquila and Priscilla (v.
26). He couldn't appear as an authorized Christian teacher until
he had been in some way integrated into the apostolic fellow-

ship. He was so effective that those who were already Christians wrote their fellow followers of "The Way" in Achaia to have them welcome him (v. 27). Apollos would build upon Paul's work. He vigorously proved from the Jewish Scriptures that Jesus is the Messiah (v. 28).

May we earn our heavenly Father's love by being good missionaries, fully conformed to God's will!

Monday, Seventh Week of Easter

Ac 19:1-8; Jn 16:29-33

Between Jesus and the World, Jesus Won

Loneliness is a fairly common but rarely welcome experience. The painter Edward Hopper vividly identified it as an all-American trait. Like the painters of the "Ashcan School," he captured the phenomenon of loneliness in everyday urban scenes. Such of his works as "House by the Railroad" and "Room in Brooklyn" show withdrawn anonymous figures and stern geometric forms that create an inescapable sense of the loneliness of persons and objects within their environment. This isolation was heightened by his characteristic use of light to insulate persons and objects in space, whether in the harsh morning light ("Early Sunday Morning" [1930]) or the eerie light of several characters in an all-night coffee stand ("Nighthawks" [1942]).

Loneliness is what Jesus felt in today's Gospel. In one last twist of misunderstanding, the disciples thought that they had grasped what Jesus had been teaching them — but they didn't. Yet they asserted that Jesus was speaking plainly, with no veiled language (v. 29). They did make out at least his statement that he was going to leave the world and go to his heavenly Father.

But, as Jesus told them, their faith was not yet complete. They didn't really understand the way in which he was to depart and be glorified. They confessed only the first part of the pattern: that Jesus had come from the heavenly Father (v. 30). Their expression of confidence paralleled St. Peter's unfounded claim that he was ready to die for Jesus, made during this same farewell of Jesus to his disciples at the Last Supper

Jesus met their claims with the observation that they would be scattered (v. 32), a reference to the disciples' flight at what would be the time of his most intense suffering and greatest need: in Gethsemane, in his Passion, and on the cross. Nevertheless, at the same time Jesus affirmed (v. 33) that he had conquered the world. His crucifixion would be a victory over those who were hostile to him. The disciples showed that they'd come part of the way to a proper understanding of Jesus, but they still hadn't fully grasped the significance of his departure. Jesus' victory over the world enabled him to promise the gift of peace to his failing and troubled disciples.

Jesus reminded them, too, that his heavenly Father was with him (v. 32). We need to keep those words before us. Our heavenly Father is always with us and, where the Father is, there too is Jesus and the Holy Spirit. God knows that loneliness can be assuaged by company, so the Holy Trinity keeps us company by dwelling within us.

The divine trinity of Father, Son, and Holy Spirit was with St. Paul. The gifted Apollos had become an innocent cause of the factions at Corinth, which Paul denounced (1 Cor 1-4). Paul had stayed in Corinth for eighteen months; today's first reading took place while he was in Ephesus, where he stayed for over two years. When Paul arrived at Ephesus, this extensive traveler for the Lord and great organizer took care that everything should proceed regularly in the churches he founded. He asked the disciples there whether they had received the Holy Spirit (v. 2). In the same religious state of initiation as Apollos, they answered that they had never even heard that there is a Holy Spirit. Their baptism was from John the Baptist (v. 3), which meant that, despite their considering themselves followers of Jesus, they were in essence followers of the Baptist. They hadn't understood the Baptist's designation of Jesus as the one for whom he was merely preparing the way. Their Christianity was immature — almost to an inconceivable degree. They stood in the "vestibule" of Christ's Church.

But St. Luke, the author of this reading from the Acts of the Apostles, suppresses any rivalry between the Baptist's movement and Jesus', just as he had avoided suggesting any rivalry between Apollos and Paul. The Baptist's followers' very obedience to him required faith in Jesus, which the Baptist had preached (v. 4). So now they were baptized with Jesus' baptism. When Paul laid his hands on them, the Holy Spirit came upon them and they spoke in tongues and prophesied (v. 5). This doesn't mean that human beings control the Holy Spirit, but that this gift is bestowed on the Church, which began at Jerusalem with the first outpouring of the Spirit and is represented by accredited witnesses.

The world, with its noise and confusion and charms, attracts our attention, but in its face-off with Jesus, Jesus won, is winning, and will win!

Tuesday, Seventh Week of Easter

Ac 20:17-27; Jn 17:1-11

Glory Be to God!

Can you imagine yourself being present in the scene of today's Gospel? It's the night before Jesus died. Aware of his fate on the next day, he prayed. He prayed both to be heard and to be overheard — heard by his heavenly Father, overheard by his Apostles and us. His prayer was essentially for his Church, asking his Father to complete within it what He had begun.

The key word in today's powerful, poignant prayer which brings Jesus' Last Supper discourse to its climactic conclusion is "glory." Six times Jesus mentions it. He asks his heavenly Father to give glory to him so he in turn may give glory back to the Father, he sums up his entire message as giving glory on earth to his Father in heaven, and he acknowledges that he has been glorified in his disciples.

The word "glory" essentially refers to the awesome, wonderful presence of God in heaven and on earth. A simplistic concept of glory to God was had by a little girl who walked daily to and from her elementary school. One day, while school was being let out, winds whipped up, along with thunder and lightning across the sky. The girl's mother, concerned that her daughter might be frightened as she walked home and herself fearful that the electric storm might harm her child, got into her car and drove to the school. The thunder roared like a thousand guns, and lightning cut through the sky like flaming swords. Soon the mother saw her daughter, and noticed that at each flash of lightning, the child would stop, look up, and smile. When she called her daughter over to the car, she asked, "What were you doing?" The child answered, "God keeps taking pictures of me."

Glory to God keeps echoing every time we celebrate the Eucharist. In the beginning of the Mass we say, "Glory to God in the highest; ... we praise you for your glory." We salute the Gospel reading with the response, "Glory to you, O Lord." In our profession of faith, we renew our belief that Jesus "will come again in glory" and we reaffirm our faith in the Holy Spirit who is "worshiped and glorified with the Father and the Son." At the preparation of the gifts for the Eucharistic celebration, we ask that the Lord accept our offering "for the praise and glory of his name." At the heart of the Eucharistic Prayer we proclaim the mystery of faith by petitioning, "Lord Jesus, come in glory." The final petition of the Eucharistic Prayer is, "We hope to enjoy forever the vision of your glory." We conclude the Eucharistic Prayer with the rousing words, "Through him... all glory and honor is yours, almighty Father, forever and ever."

Yet glory to God is more and more omitted from our public lives. A notable exception was Darrell Scott, the father of Rachel Scott, a victim of the Columbine High School shootings on April 20, 1999, in Littleton, Colorado. He was invited to address the United States House of Representatives Judiciary Committee's subcommittee. They weren't prepared for what he said. Among other things, he said:

"I am here today to declare that Columbine was not just a tragedy — it was a spiritual event that should be forcing us to look at where the real blame lies! Much of the blame lies here in this room.... Spiritual presences were within our educational systems for most of our nation's history. What has happened to us as a nation? We have refused to honor God, and in so doing, we open the doors to hatred and violence.... We do not need more restrictive laws. We do need a change of heart and a humble acknowledgment that this nation was founded on the principle of simple trust in God!"

Jesus begins his prayer at the Last Supper with placing his whole being before God. Then he asks for the consummation of God's glory and of his own glorification: to bring eternal life into the human story by making God known.

By eternal life Jesus means not the *duration* of life, but the *quality* of life. This consists in knowing the true God (v. 3). In our age of facts and information on every subject imaginable, what does it mean "to *know*"? To know in the biblical sense denotes *intimate* experience of someone, as when Genesis speaks of Adam knowing Eve his wife, with the result that she conceived (Gn 4:1). There's no doubt that *intellectual* grasp of Christian teachings plays a role in faith — but, alone, that doesn't lead to eternal life.

What does it mean, especially, to know *God*? Jesus speaks

of the God whom he had taught us to call "Father." In fact, Jesus had intimately called Him "Abba": "Daddy." Jesus prays that all who call themselves disciples will come to know himself. The person who really knows Jesus as the one who reveals God as Father enjoys life. The context in which Jesus speaks shows that by knowing God he also means giving God glory by joining with him in finishing the work that the heavenly Father has given us to do on earth (v. 4).

In today's reading from the Acts of the Apostles, St. Luke, its author, presents St. Paul at the conclusion of his career as the great missionary and pastor. This first section recalls Paul's past ministry in Ephesus, registers his feelings about what lies ahead, and testifies to his faithful accomplishment of his ministry. Paul's statement that he considered his life to have value only to the extent that he might finish the ministry that he received from the Lord Jesus sums up his concept of the whole meaning of life.

Today, the lure of danger and the potential for *personal* glory are powerful. When, in 1913, Sir Ernest Shackleton needed a crew for his planned expedition across the Antarctic, he announced his intentions in *The Times* of London. "Men wanted for hazardous journey," one notice read. "Small wages, bitter cold, long months of complete darkness, safe return doubtful. Honor and recognition in case of success." That announcement drew more than 5,000 replies. And every few years, when the word goes out, thousands of Americans submit applications to NASA, hoping to embark upon risky travel by rocket.

Paul's desire to give glory to God is a restatement of Jesus' attitude. In the face of uncertainty about the future, both Paul and Jesus could say from their heart that they had done their very best. An old poster said, "Be patient with me — God isn't finished with me yet!" In many areas the world, too, doesn't look finished. We have much work to do to give glory to God.

Ac 20:28-38; Jn 17:11-19

True Friendship

Today's Gospel, the same as last Sunday's, which is from Jesus' farewell discourse, presents part of his sublime priestly prayer, in which he consecrates all who will carry on his work. It's our golden privilege to be able to eavesdrop on his personal appeal on behalf of his friends and followers. Jesus, departing this world, leaves behind disciples so that they may continue to reveal him. He prays that the heavenly Father protect his fragile disciples, who are sent into the world as he had been sent.

Jesus' prayer has four key ideas.

The first is protection for his followers in a hostile world (vv. 11f.): Jesus would remain with his followers forever and defend them whenever the going gets rough. For that, he wants us to be one, as he and his heavenly Father are one.

The second concept is the world. On this, Jesus is paradoxical. On one hand, God so loved the world that He gave His only Son, the lamb who would take away the world's sins. On the other hand, the world is a kind of Satan which is opposed to everything that Jesus' mission represents.

Jesus continues to be concerned over his followers' *involvement* in the world. Involvement is necessary. The ancient Greek statesman Pericles said that just because you don't take an interest in politics doesn't mean politics won't take an interest in you. Involvement, though, has two extremes. One is to become so involved in the world that we forget our values and accept the world's. The other is to flee from the world — a position that overemphasizes the evil of the world and forgets God's love for it. Christian apostleship means not a withdrawal from life, but becoming better equipped for life; not a release from problems, but a way to solve problems; not an easy peace, but a triumphant warfare; and not an avoidance of troubles, but facing and conquering them.

A third key concept for Jesus' followers is joy — *Jesus'* joy. Even those who are suffering have an instinctive awareness of their need for a *joyful* message, and the message of Jesus is in the final analysis the only real, lasting, deep joy that the world can know.

In the fourth and last concept in Jesus' prayer (v. 19), he mentions a very important aspect of life — *truth*. He speaks of his followers as being *consecrated* (literally "made holy") in truth (Greek *aletheia*, "unconcealment" or "revelation," removal of a veil). We can be *dedicated* to *anything*: a job, a cause, a nation. But *consecration* requires that we trust more in grace than in our personal capabilities. Sometimes today, in the Church as well as in our lives, there is instead the opposite of revelation: concealment, unwillingness to face the truth, "killing the messenger."

St. John the Evangelist wrote his reminder of Jesus' message at the end of the first century — when there was a need for formulating the identity of the Church, for realizing the unity of the local churches with each other and with Jesus' total Church, and for the comprehension that Jesus really empowered the Church to continue doing what he had done.

The Apostles were anxious, especially in the time of their life which we commemorate these days — that time before the Holy Spirit came on the first Pentecost (which we commemorate next Sunday). It probably didn't dawn on the Apostles for a long time what their mission in life should be. Nor did they know exactly what the Church should be.

One of those who had ideas of where things should go was St. Paul who, of course, entered the Church a little later. In today's first reading (which continues from yesterday), we see part of the touching scene of his final meeting with friends and leaders of the Church in Ephesus. Paul was on his way to Jerusalem toward the end of his ministry. Paul's teaching came from his heart, and he spoke with strong emotion — even to the point of tears. This section of the discourse addresses the sacredness of the charge which pastors have received, the threatening dangers that demand watchfulness, and a commendation of pastors to God.

The elders were to remember Paul's blood and tears, his hard manual labor, and his tireless preaching of the Gospel. He sternly warned them to carefully shepherd the flock, to avoid avarice, and to be generous. He charged them to keep watch for wolves who would lead the flock astray. After shared words of inspiration and encouragement, he prayed with the presbyters of Ephesus and embraced them. Grieved by the thought of never seeing one another again, Paul and his sailing companions had to turn themselves away from those who stayed.

We read about Paul being many things — tireless missioner, mostly, but also courageous pioneer, fearless apologist, evangelist, and teacher — yet we rarely read about him as devoted friend. Scenes like today's reveal that Paul understood friendship well. This is an important lesson because today friendship seems to be a lost virtue in many parts of our society.

Let's take from today's readings an awareness of Jesus' protection of us, an inner joy, a proper love for the world, a constant search for truth, and — as given the example by Jesus and Paul — the nature of true friendship.

Thursday, Seventh Week of Easter

Ac 22:30, 23:6-11; Jn 17:20-26

Let's All Be One, for Christ's Sake!

Jesus' prayer at the Last Supper ended as it began: solemnly, intimately, in the hearing of friends, with many references to love, and filled with hope. In the first part of his prayer (vv. 1-8), Jesus had prayed for himself, in the second part (vv. 9-19) for his disciples, and in the last part — today's — for us and all believers.

Jesus was praying that a oneness among those who believe in him might make God known.

The entire section is called Jesus' High Priestly Prayer, because in it he consecrates his body and blood for the sacrifice in which they're about to be offered and because in it he gives his blessings to the Church that he's about to bring forth.

Jesus here comes to the pinnacle of his petitions: that all may be one. We have to be reminded of the need for oneness: we often witness breakdowns of communication in families, enmity among members of the same faith community, dissension in civil society, and hostility between nations. Jesus' oneness is to overcome all such divisions, especially those within the fold. He wants a unity like that between himself and the Father. That union of the Father and the Son is heart speaking to heart. Its key is love.

Today's portion begins (v. 20) with Jesus praying for those who will believe in him through the Apostles' word. It's been said that the only Gospel some people will read is the way Jesus' followers live. Denominationalism and sectarianism among Christians are among the world's greatest scandals. Unless we in the Church have the unity willed by God, we can't perform the Church's essential mission: that the world may believe (v. 21). That we may be one, as Jesus and the heavenly Father are one, Jesus has given us the glory which the Father gave him (v. 22). When Christians preserve God's unity in love that Jesus has given, we're the continuation of Christ as mediator and revealer of God: we show the world that he was sent by God (v. 23).

Jesus concludes his prayer (v. 25) with confidence that his heavenly Father will deal rightly with those who have accepted the revelation of God in him. Even as death approaches, he sounds the note of triumph that he shall live and, through the Paraclete who is to come, will continue to make known God's name (v. 26).

If there's only one God, and He has revealed Himself in Jesus Christ, why has He allowed so many religions? Pope John Paul

II wrote (*Crossing the Threshold of Hope* [New York: Alfred A. Knopf, 1994]) that instead of marveling at the fact that Providence allows such a great variety of religions, we should be amazed at the number of common elements within them.

And Vatican Council II (*Nostra Aetate*, #2) said: "The Catholic Church rejects nothing that is true and holy in these religions. The Church has a high regard for their conduct and way of life, for those precepts and doctrines which, although differing on many points from that which the Church believes and propounds, often reflects a ray of that truth which enlightens all men. However, the Church proclaims, and is bound to proclaim, that Christ is 'the way and the truth and the life' (Jn 1:6)." The same document (#3) urges all to "work toward mutual understanding as well as toward the preservation and promotion of social justice, moral welfare, peace, and freedom for the benefit of all mankind."

We have a special relationship with other Christian sects. These have a long history, mostly starting in the sixteenth century, when they broke from Roman Catholicism over scandals in the Church. They still retain their allegiance to Jesus Christ and his teachings as they see them. They deserve our acknowledgment, respect, and cooperation in all areas of benefit to the human race. Yet there can be no Christian unity worthy of the name without sensitivity. Children were overheard inside a church admiring the stained-glass window depicting Christ at prayer. "It's beautiful here," one boy said with greater wisdom than he realized, "but it ain't no good if you're outside."

It's especially important for us to be in union with Judaism. Vatican Council II (*Nostra Aetate* #4) says: "The [Catholic] Church can not forget that she received the revelation of the Old Testament through the people with whom God, in his ineffable mercy, made the Ancient Covenant."

In this age of the global village, we must broaden our horizons for unity even further. For example, although both the theology and anthropology of Islam are very distant from Christianity, some of the most beautiful names in the human language are given to the God of the Koran. And it's impossible not to admire Muslims' fidelity to prayer and the centrality they give to the will of God.

Mindful of Asia, we can no longer be entirely Western in our approach to unity. At a time when Western banks use Eastern languages as well as Western in their transactions, the Church must do no less. Western, and especially scholastic, theology seems too rational to have adapted itself to the religions of Asia: Asians prefer to not get entangled in quarrels over words. From Asian religions in general, we can learn to be more open, receptive, sensitive, tolerant, and forgiving in the midst of a plurality of religions.

From Hindus, we can learn the practice of contemplation, renunciation of one's will, and the spirit of nonviolence. *Nostra Aetate* (#2) said: "In Hinduism men explore the divine mystery and express it through an endless bounty of myths and through penetrating philosophical insight. They seek freedom from the anguish of our human condition, either by way of the ascetic life, profound meditation, or by taking refuge in God with love and trust."

In Buddhism, "enlightenment" comes down to the conviction that the world is the source of evil and of suffering for the human race. Buddhists attempt to liberate themselves through detachment from this evil world. The culmination of the spiritual process of detachment is *nirvana*, a state of perfect indifference with regard to the world. Buddhism, although in large measure an atheistic system, offers lessons in detachment from material goods, respect for life, and compassion.

From Confucianism, we can learn filial piety, respect for elders, and humanitarianism. From Taoists come simplicity, humility, and a reverence and respect for nature. From animists, we can learn reverence and respect for nature, too, and gratitude for harvests. African and Asian animist religions stress ancestor worship. Is there, perhaps, in this veneration of ancestors a kind of preparation for the Christian "communion of saints," in which all believers whether living or dead form a single community? Inspired by today's liturgy, we pray for the cleverness of St. Paul in today's first reading. When at the behest of the Jews he appeared before the official of the Roman cohort, Paul skillfully utilized the hostility between the Pharisees and the Sadducees about belief in such things as resurrection and angels and spirits to create such a shouting chaos that the Roman official had to take him away. We pray, too, that all of us will recognize that only virtues like humility, compassion, peacemaking, and sacrifice make community.

Friday, Seventh Week of Easter
Ac 25:13-21; Jn 21:15-19

The Ways of the Holy Spirit

At an ecumenical conference for clergymen, one evening after the arduous duties of the day Father O'Connell, Reverend Wilson, and Rabbi Cohen were indulging in a friendly game of poker. Unfortunately, their excitement grew a little noisy, and a hotel detective, in a burst of overzealousness, entered the room, confiscated the chips and cards, and arrested them under the strict anti-gambling statutes of the conference town.

The magistrate before whom they appeared was embarrassed. "Gentlemen," he said, "I would rather this hadn't happened, but since you've been arrested, I can't dismiss the case without some investigation. Nevertheless, in view of your profession, I feel I can trust you to tell the truth. I won't ask for any evidence other than your words. If each of you can tell me that you weren't gambling, that would be sufficient for me and I will release you. Now, Father O'Connell?"

The worthy priest said, "Your Honor, surely it's important to be certain that we define what we mean by gambling. In a narrow, but entirely valid sense, what we describe as gambling is only truly so if there's a desire to win money. In addition, we might confine gambling to situations where the loss of money would be harmful, as otherwise such loss might merely be viewed as a variable admission fee...."

"I understand," interrupted the magistrate. "I'll take it, then, that you, Father O'Connell, weren't gambling by your definition of the word. And you, Reverend Wilson?"

The good minister straightened his tie and said, "I entirely agree with my learned colleague, Your Honor. Further, I might stress that gambling is gambling only if there are stakes involved. Admittedly, there was money on the table, but it remains to be determined whether this money would eventually have found its way into the possession of an individual who was not its owner at the start of the game, or if, in fact, it was merely being used as a convenient marker that...."

"Yes, yes," interrupted the magistrate again. "I'll accept that as satisfactory indication that you weren't gambling, Reverend Wilson. And now you, Rabbi Cohen, were you gambling?"

The pious rabbi's eyebrows shot upward. "Your Honor, with whom?"

We need cleverness in the cause of religion. Different people will exercise that cleverness differently. That was true of Sts. Peter and Paul. Today's first reading speaks of Paul. The procurator Festus (the same office as Pontius Pilate had had) related Paul's case to Herod Agrippa II, who was on a courtesy visit to Caesarea. His eagerness to see Paul was like that of Herod Antipas to see Jesus (Lk 9:9; 23:8). He in turn offered the judgment of a Roman official that the controversy between Paul and the Jews concerned certain points of their own religion and Jesus about whom Paul had preached.

Paul was perhaps too abrasive to be the leader that Peter was, but he was very capable of using the system to his own advantage. In yesterday's first reading, we saw his exploitation of the bad feelings between Pharisees and Sadducees to the point where he had them attacking each other instead of himself before the Roman official. Today, we see him exercising his rights as a Roman citizen to appeal from Caesarea in Palestine, where he was, to the emperor in Rome. As a result, he would receive at government expense a trip to Rome — where he wanted to go in the first place. This would enable him to preach in Rome for two years. Clever!

The life of the Holy Spirit in Peter was different. He had three times denied Jesus in his final suffering and, in today's Gospel reading, the risen Lord sought his love and forgave him. Jesus began by asking Peter three times whether Peter loved him — a central question of every Christian's life. Peter, however, was sad and confused. Was Jesus alluding to his sin of denying him three times and asking, "Do you love me now, at last?" Or was Jesus asking, "Do you love me more than you love your nets, your boat, and a catch of fish?" Or was he asking, "Do you love me more than your fellow disciples do?"

By now, Peter was aware that he had often left much to be desired. And he'd been made compassionate by his own need for forgiveness and mercy. Love, humility, contrition, and obedience to the Lord were to be the hallmarks of Peter's future ministry. His glorious side enabled him to grow in fidelity.

Peter would now no longer dare to say anything that would put him above the rest: no bold claims, no rash promises. He couldn't even answer with the same word for "love" that Jesus used. In asking Peter if he loved him, Jesus' word — *agapas* in the Greek of John's Gospel — connoted sacrifice, and Peter remembered that after his previous grandiose promise to lay down his life for Jesus he had denied Jesus three times. So, unsure of whether he was capable of that highest kind of love, he answered by affirming, in the Gospel's original Greek, *philo*. This meant a love of sentiment, of affection, of attachment. Of those he was sure.

Upon Peter's affirmative reply, the consequences of true love followed: *responsibility* and *sacrifice.* Jesus indicated Peter's *responsibility* by directing him to feed his lambs and his sheep. He was making Peter his great shepherd. As for *sacrifice.* Jesus predicted that Peter's love would involve the greatest sacrifice of all: his life. Peter may not have been clever, like Paul, in using the system and traveling widely for Christ — but his determination to follow the Lord and to lead the Apostles enabled him to be the first head of the Church.

For us, as for Peter and Paul, recognition of the extent of our love for Jesus often comes slowly, but we have all, like them, responded in love. For us as for them, that involves responsibility, self-sacrifice, and perhaps suffering. One benefit of reverses like suffering is that they make sure we don't get too comfortable and miss opportunities. In life, as in sports, if there's no opponent there's no game. Jesus' Resurrection shows that through suffering and death one can achieve triumph.

Peter and Paul both exhibit the strengthening effect of the Holy Spirit, differently for each. The Holy Spirit, like the sunshine which spreads over land and sea and yet is present to all people as though it were for them alone, redirected Paul's fire and channeled Peter's leadership and stability. And the Holy Spirit showers God's grace on each of us. The Spirit, whose special arrival at the first Pentecost we shall celebrate next Sunday, enables all of us to discern, clarify, and develop our personal gifts, so that we can live as God intended.

So let's seize the day (*carpe diem,* as the ancients used to say). Too many people put off something that brings them joy just because they don't get around to it. We'll go back and visit the grandparents when we get Stevie toilet-trained. We'll entertain when we replace the living-room carpet. We'll go on a second honeymoon when we get two more kids out of college.

Do we run through each day on the fly? When we ask, "How

are you?", do we hear the reply? Twenty years from now we will
be more disappointed by the things we didn't do than by the ones
we did. So let's sail away from our safe harbor and catch the trade
winds in our sails. Explore. Dream.

Saturday, Seventh Week of Easter
Ac 28:16-20, 30f.; Jn 21:20-25

The Truth About the Life of Jesus

Both of our readings for today, the last day of the Easter season,
are epilogues of the two books we've been reading most during
this Easter season: St. Luke's Acts of the Apostles and the Gospel of St. John.

In our Gospel reading, St. Peter's question about the Beloved
Disciple, St. John, derives from a saying going around that the
Beloved Disciple wasn't going to die. The misunderstanding is
answered by Jesus (v. 22) and by the narrator (vv. 23f.).

The question shows again the intimate association of Peter
and John. Just as John had questioned Jesus at the Last Supper
to satisfy the curiosity of Peter, so Peter questions Jesus here
about the welfare of John. Jesus' answer was, in brief, that John's
destiny was none of Peter's business.

The very last verse of John's Gospel, about the many other
things that Jesus did which the whole world wouldn't be able to
contain (which may have been added by another hand), indicates
that John, like the other evangelists, selected only those signs
about Jesus that were suited to his purpose in writing. John wrote
to show that Jesus was God, that God is love, and that to his followers Jesus offers divine life.

Today's first reading from the Acts of the Apostles shows

St. Paul in prison in Rome. He would have to stay in his assigned lodging with his wrist chained to that of his guard, who would be changed frequently — a degree of freedom granted to prisoners who weren't considered dangerous. This mild form of custody for Paul reflects, perhaps, the arrangements made for him by Festus, governor in Palestine, to whom Paul's trial seemed senseless and from whom Paul had appealed to go to Rome.

Rome had an important Jewish community, which had gradually and painfully regrouped after the expulsion of Jews by the Emperor Claudius in A.D. 49. The two full years that Paul stayed in his lodgings in Rome (Ac 28:30) were roughly A.D. 61-63. When Paul speaks of himself as having been handed over to the Romans (v. 17), he's making Jesus' trial echo in his own.

Paul's first act in Rome was to learn from the leaders of the Jewish community whether the Jews of Jerusalem planned to pursue their case against him before the civil jurisdiction of Rome. Paul told the Roman Jews that he had no accusation to make against his fellow Jews (v. 19). Although unfaithful Israel had made itself Paul's adversary, Paul was no adversary of Israel, but the beleaguered exponent of its hope, the Messiah (v. 20). That hope referred, at least primarily, to Jesus' Resurrection; a second reference is to the "ingathering" that's effected by the proclamation of the resurrected Christ. That process was still under way in Rome.

When Paul presented his case to the Jews, they answered (v. 21) that they hadn't received any recommendations about him from Jerusalem. Distracted by national troubles and aware of the weakness of their case, the authorities in Jerusalem had sent no instructions to Rome regarding Paul, but the local Jews of the Diaspora in Rome must have heard of his work.

They arranged to come to his lodgings (v. 23); they came in great numbers, and from morning to night Paul expounded his position to them. Some were convinced. To those who didn't arrive at belief, Paul cited Isaiah (vv. 26f., from Is 6:9f.) to reject them. He went to the Gentiles to proclaim Jesus' message. That he preached and taught there (v. 31) means that his argument was continuous. He was giving the indomitable Christian message in the center of what was the world-conquering power at the time.

The epilogue of the Book of Acts captures the whole of Paul's career: proclaiming the kingdom of God and teaching about the Lord with boldness. We see Paul's personal fate overshadowed by an open-ended triumph of the Gospel over its powerful opposition. But that, after all, rather than the "acts of the apostles," was the real subject matter of the book all along. The plan of the risen Lord for his witnesses is complete at vv. 30-31. It refers back to Jesus at the time of his Ascension telling his disciples that they would witness to him in Jerusalem, throughout Judea and Samaria, and to the ends of the earth (1:8).

So the Acts of the Apostles closes on a note of triumph. Paul is free to preach to all who came to him, and the Jews seem to have let the case go by default. Many details of these two prison years — two years! — in Rome are found in the "Epistles of the Captivity" (Colossians, Ephesians, Philemon, and Philippians, written in that order in about A.D. 63). These all show that Paul expected to be released. They also stress the doctrine of the Mystical Body of Christ.

The end of an epoch was reached when Paul, the last of the witnesses commissioned by the risen Lord, completed his missionary odyssey from Jerusalem, the city of the true Israel's first assembly, to Rome, the center of a vast and fertile world of the Gentiles.

It's the exalted Christ, the true prophet of salvation to all the nations, whose path has been plotted in the Acts of the Apostles; his witnesses have come and gone in its pages. Further glory to God in Jesus would take place beginning with the first Pentecost, which we celebrate tomorrow. Through the imagery of tongues of fire and rushing winds, God's Spirit comes as an unexpected and incredible energy let loose upon an unsuspecting world.

The first Pentecost is the story of new creation and new possibility as hope triumphs over desolation and loss. It's easy to forget that this was but a beginning. The fact that we know the end of the story, the triumphant spreading of the Gospel to the very ends of the known world, can take away from the real miracle which Luke seeks to record.

Perhaps the most intriguing aspect of the Third Person of the Trinity is that the Holy Spirit has no face. Father and Son are described in ways that invite a degree of imaginative engagement. The Spirit can't be envisaged in that way. There's something intrinsically mysterious and indefinable about the Holy Spirit. The Spirit is more like an activity that's dynamic, creative, and moving.

Like the wind, the Holy Spirit blows sometimes with devastating power through the landscape; like human breath, that wind is the sign of life, an outward sign of the most intimate of all divine gifts. In the Bible, Spirit is often a name for that mysterious God-given energy which generates new life in unexpected ways and unexpected places. With that sound from heaven, "like the rush of a mighty wind," the concept of the world we have carefully ordered for ourselves was turned upside down.

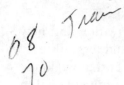